Fleeting Moments
Praying When You Are Too Busy

Fleeting Moments

Praying When You Are Too Busy

Loretta Pehanich

CONTENTS

Thankfully, this book is short.

I'm sure you are too busy

for anything longer...

Dedicated to my husband Steve

Foreword

Thank you a thousand times over to the good people who helped me to the insights I present in this work.

Spiritual directors, published writers, friends, and family members influenced this guide. You will read paraphrases of Scripture passages, and perhaps some ideas will sound familiar. You might even hear echoes of thoughts from great saints.

I cannot take credit, except for managing the self-discipline to sit and write when the vocation to be a writer called. While this book comes from my own experience, it grew from the inspiration from others.

I have discovered that "too busy" can mean that I have not prioritized time for something. Rather than say, "I'm too busy!" it is more honest for me to say, "You know, I just have not prioritized that undertaking high enough on my list right now to allow me to complete it."

It is okay. As I struggle to reprioritize, it helps to measure the current event against the long-term goal. I find myself backsliding, too, into the urgent demands that tempt me to displace what is important.

To all of us who travel the busy road, we do not travel alone. We've got lots of company. And most important, God is with us.

"You are busy about many things.

But there is need of only one thing..."

Luke 10:42-42

Introduction

I would have written this book years ago, but I've been too busy!

My friends and I once facetiously formed the "Too Busy Club," where to qualify for membership you had to miss at least three meetings in a row, or you weren't busy enough to be a member.

How can a person find time, or make time, to pray? What do you do when you can't find any words?

Retirees complain that they are busier than they ever were while working. As people age, their pace slows down a bit, so time actually does shrink for people. The 20 seconds it used to take to tie one's shoes now takes 40 seconds. Such subtle changes occur without people realizing when their days got shorter.

Young people have full agendas with classes, careers, causes and relationships as they start out to build independent lives. Our culture offers many pursuits that keep young professionals and students running at full throttle.

Parents are also extremely busy. As society moves toward better equality between genders, more men are experiencing the hectic lifestyle traditionally ascribed to women. Parenting is more of a shared experience than what it was in the '50s and '60s. Men are ironing, cooking, shuttling kids, and filling their days with to do's like never before. Both genders seek a stronger spirituality as they push kids out the door.

Raising four kids while working full time, I discovered that time is elastic depending upon how you choose to use it. For example, moments of pondering while I waited at a park for a piano lesson to end became a treasured half hour. I can still see that tree stretched above me as I marveled at God's gifts to me. While the children occupied themselves, I was allowed to have a timeless moment—a blessed and free gift of respite with God. That afternoon stays with me, years later, as I recall that special moment of reflection.

We've all had the opposite experience as well: at the end of a day you wonder where the time went. The activities done are a blur. It feels as if someone pulled a rug out from under you.

Time out. How can people take it? I remember one of many disheartening conversations that occurred when I was running home from Boy Scouts—or was it Girl Scouts—and I was driving the carpool by way of the library for someone's critical assignment. One of our darlings said, "I need poster board for my science project."

"Couldn't you have remembered that while we were on our way back from that last errand?"

Moments flee past.

A financial planner and committed Catholic was curious about this book. "Why pray anyway?" he asked. This basic question caught me by surprise, but it got me thinking. When we set out to pray, *why* are we doing it? Is there something we want to "achieve" by praying? Is there a benefit to praying? So, before you go another sentence, ask yourself: "*Why* do I pray, or why do

I want to squeeze a few more moments of prayer into my life?"
Examine your motives. You may discover that you are seeking

- *More peace of mind*
- *Relief from stress*
- *Help with making a decision*
- *Clarity about what is important in life*
- *A closer relationship with God.*

These and many, many other reasons draw people to pray. And of course, busy people probably have a list of reasons why we are *not* praying.

This list may include one or more of the following:

- *No time.*
- *No established habit.*
- *No idea how to start.*
- *Fear. What if God wants me to change something?*
- *Apathy. Things are good enough as they are.*
- *Control. If I get closer to God, what will God ask of me?*
- *Contentment. I like my life, for the most part, as it is.*

List your own reasons why you find it difficult to pray or to pray in the way your insides seem to be longing for. Identifying "the problem" or the crux of the situation is a huge step towards changing it.

We have to start somewhere, somehow, to seek peace. One option, they say, is to prioritize. How I hate that word when other people tell me I just have to do a better job of prioritizing!

As if all the things I want to do in my life will fit in if I somehow just try a little harder.

Do you have stacks of mail piling up on the counter as you save that new catalogue to read later (is it too early to be thinking of Christmas giving)? Do you hope to review that appeal for donations (after all, how can you throw away catchy envelopes and beautiful appeals, sight unseen?). We all have to process a stream of paperwork from bills to flyers to notes about neighborhood events. Magazine subscriptions are down, maybe because households still have seven issues of their favorite magazines waiting to be read.

Another option is letting go. Some of us expect to accomplish a long list of items that only a superhero could manage in a single day. Is it possible to learn to let go of long lists? As one wise person once said to me, the Savior of the world already came, and it wasn't you.

What bothers me about being too busy is the sensation of being enslaved to demands that I cannot control. And I love to be in control! A list of items successfully completed gives me the illusion that I alone have the power of accomplishment.

> *How does a person in the modern world create a meaningful prayer life when the ancient masters of prayer prescribe uninterrupted quiet periods and efforts to do nothing?*

And prayer? How does a person with a to-do list the size of North America feel comfortable sitting still long enough to listen to God speak? And reading—even if it is the Bible or written prayers in some inspirational book—can feel like so much more *work*.

People wonder what falls into the realm of prayer. They may have grown up thinking that prayer must be formal, or memorized, or take place only in holy places. Such concepts can be very limiting. To steal an idea from Saint Paul's first letter to the Corinthians, it's time to put aside childhood views. We need to think bigger about prayer.

But how does a person in the modern world create a meaningful prayer life when the ancient masters of prayer prescribe uninterrupted quiet periods and efforts to *do* nothing? Some of us simply have no idea what to do should "free time" appear. "I can't stand when I have nothing to do," one busy person confided. Doing nothing is countercultural. And there's the temptation to reach for a cell phone or electronic option when a spare moment surfaces.

Much of what we do already can be transformed easily into prayer. And many of the actions we perform now *are* prayer, but we don't recognize them as such. As the old adage says, "actions speak louder than words." As you read on, I hope you grow in awareness of the ways you are praying already. In addition, we can make slight alterations that turn into prayers these actions that are speaking so loudly. A small course correction that changes our trajectory can lead to a completely different end result.

> *If you haven't made much time for prayer in your life yet, don't be discouraged! Embrace hope. You can achieve the richer life you wish for.*

If you haven't made much time for prayer in your life yet, don't be discouraged! Embrace hope. You can achieve the richer life you wish for.

My son calls me the multitasking master. As I smile, I wonder if I am a victim of a self-imposed multi-taskmaster. As I talk on a Bluetooth while driving and fumble for a pen to jot a quick note, I become a danger to myself and others. Not taking a few moments for prayer can also put me on a road to disaster.

Perhaps some of the ideas and prayers in this book will lead you to enjoy a moment of prayer. Perhaps God's grace will abound and open a door for you to a blessed new prayer practice, or a deeper, more fruitful prayer life overall. That is my hope!

A guarantee

I can guarantee you that God is longing for a deeper relationship with you. Prayer is a means to that relationship.

I cannot guarantee that the suggestions in these pages will resonate in your soul, but perhaps they will spark your creativity and open new avenues to assist you in seeking more fully the God who loves all busy people.

Chapter 1

Now is the moment: Getting started

Beginnings can be difficult. Do you put off beginning?

What if today you were to begin something: to carve out a fleeting moment of prayer from the tumult of your day— not for God, or for someone else, but for your own wholeness?

I know a woman who felt too busy to tackle the daunting task of engaging in conversation with the Almighty. She had an invisible gremlin nagging at her, "Who do you think you are to dare to seek a conversation with the Lord and Master of the Universe?"

It is no wonder that she put off praying. And no wonder she intended to make time later and judged her efforts as not good enough when she did slow down long enough to pray.

Beginnings can be difficult if we approach a 500-page volume, but easy if we decide to read just one page. It can be intimidating for a busy person to resolve to change from a prayer life that leaves them wanting more. We succumb to the common tendency to impose on ourselves an ambitious plan that requires action every day. This is hard for a busy person to sustain.

This book does not contain 365 suggestions on how to pray. That could just tempt the busy person to feel another pressure to yet another draining commitment. And that might just result in more self-recrimination for not meeting a goal you set for yourself.

Busy people moving from a spotty practice of prayer to a consistent dedication to prayer may feel guilty when they skip a day. That could lead them to judging themselves negatively and to giving up. Schedules are fine, but when it comes to prayer, too rigid a schedule can make me feel guilty over uncompleted tasks. Good intentions can steal away my peace of mind when a schedule for a quality prayer time every day falls short.

So how does a busy person pray? Relax. Just take a deep breath. Right now, before reading the next sentence. Did you do it? Something about breath connects to the One who hovered over the waters of creation and breathed on them (Genesis 1:2). A slow, deep, conscious breath can be a prayer. It is as simple as that. You have begun.

> *If this sounds silly, you may be busier than you think.*

If once a day you take a deep breath with the idea of connecting to the One Great Breather, a habit can form. If one breath is manageable, try two. If this sounds silly, you may be busier than you think. One of the hardest things for busy people to do is to slow down. A slow breath really can work wonders. So take a prayer breath now.

When you hear yourself thinking, "I barely have time to breathe," that is the time to turn your next breath into a prayer. "Jesus!" You can speak it under your breath with desperation. Or you can breathe this holy name as a quiet remembrance of God's great love for you. There is power in the name of Jesus. Adding it to your next breath may not yield instantaneous stress relief, but it makes a difference somehow, as time moves ahead. Is there a reason why the words breath and breadth are so similar? Perhaps a deep breath will bring about a connection to the breadth of God's limitless love.

There's no one "right" way to pray

There are as many different ways to pray as there are people. Prayer is a relationship with God, and no two relationships are identical.

When you make a new acquaintance, you begin building bridges through activities, conversations, activities, and time together that eventually create a network of connections, also known as a relationship. You talk. You listen.

Relating to God is no different. We grow closer to God over time. So please don't discount your own experience out of hand as something that "doesn't measure up."

And don't underestimate your skill at listening. Some people may find it hard to believe that God can speak to us via our dreams, the random thoughts that pop into our heads, a casual remark made by a stranger, a few notes from a song, a sentence in a novel, and an emotional tug in your gut. Yet God does indeed "speak" to our souls using all these methods, and many more.

God can use anything to reach us, including our minds, will, emotions, memories, and imaginations. God also uses our bodies, our work, our actions and the actions of others. Here are some examples from other busy people, indicating various means God uses to grab us:

- *"I had a dream last night where I was walking on the beach, without a care in the world. When I woke up, I just felt a great sense of peace."*

- *"The character in that novel beat his chest and said, 'Here is where the sky is blue,' and I knew somewhere deep inside that I want to be that kind of person—someone who sees beauty even when circumstances are grey."*
- *"I couldn't get that one line from Sunday's homily out of my mind..."*
- *"I felt sick to my stomach when I saw the photo of the child dying of starvation."*
- *"Suddenly I remembered a scene from my childhood that encouraged me now to keep going."*

Sometimes we think God is silent, but actually we have been too busy to realize that we are not listening. Or we listened for half a minute, moved into our day without a backward glance, and quickly forgot an inspiring insight. Or, to paraphrase 1 Samuel 3:7, we are constantly praying: "Listen, Lord, your servant is speaking!"

Busy people attempting to grow in their prayer life will make progress by paying attention. I find that if I can cultivate an awareness of how outside influences or people are affecting me, I will notice God at work more often. And believe it: noticing God, too, is prayer.

Many people have days when prayer finds them without any prior stimulus. God reaches out to them in such fleeting moments, providing grace that cannot be predicted, captured, or contained.

God uses a speeding ticket?

One busy executive told the story of the day a police officer pulled her over for speeding. She was mortified, and wishing that she wasn't culpable for her driving. As the police officer took her license back to his car, she waited in silence. Cars streaked past. As she waited, she had a divine insight expressed not in words, but in some sort of sense coming from deep within: God was inviting her to slow down.

Her experience is not odd or aberrant. God doesn't reserve himself for just a select few, or communicate only to prophets of old or exceptionally holy people. God seeks to be close to every one of us. God does deal with each of us uniquely, depending upon what we need.

God is able to find us wherever we are hiding, even if we took no prior action to invite God to "speak" to us. God is the great initiator and Master of prayer. So try a very simple prayer again: relax and breathe.

Perhaps you grew up with a definition of prayer as something formal, or rote, or clearly defined and tied in a neat package. Although Merriam-Webster may define prayer as "an address (as a petition) to God in word or thought or a set order of words used in praying, or an earnest request or wish," this is too narrow. And it's all one sided—as if I control everything that happens. Prayer is not one more thing to check off on your to-do list. St. Ignatius of Loyola taught that prayer— at the heart of it— is relationship and therefore involves both speaking and listening.

> *Prayer is not one more thing to check off on your to-do list.*

Prayer can be a conversation with God. It also can be just like sitting silently with a friend, neither of you saying a thing. Prayer is primarily God's project, and we are willing participants. Sometimes, all we have to do is be there. Remember, you are God's work of art. [1]

---

[1] "We are God's handiwork." Ephesians 2:10.

Perhaps you already have a habit of starting your day with a prayer that you have loved for years, or one that began to sing in your heart recently. This is something to build upon. Most people find it worthwhile to return to a prayer that bore fruit yesterday, like savoring cheesecake left over from last night's party. A previous moment that drew you closer to God has the potential to take you there again. And being busy people, isn't it easy to stick with what works, rather than feeling a need to reinvent something new every day? As a spiritual director told me, "Let Christ lead." It is best to discover just how God wants to speak to us personally each day.

> *Return to a prayer that bore fruit yesterday, like savoring cheesecake left over from last night's party.*

The secret is to be willing to pause in a hectic moment when, from out of the blue, an insight does come, and one that is clearly not from the present activities. If God's peace pops into your day, accept it with gratitude. And perhaps a quick deep breath.

Sometimes when you least expect it, you will encounter a quote or a verse from a song that reminds you of God's unfailing love. You may stumble upon ideas that have helped others feel alive and joyful at prayer. If you ask God to be present and to reveal God's presence to you, be ready, and pay attention. It may even be a paragraph in a newspaper, for example, that inspires you. Now if only you could remember it!

So as you figure out how a busy person prays, buy yourself a notebook, with pockets where you can stuff notes and sources of encouragement that you encounter from other people. Maybe a graphic or photo in a magazine tugs at your heart and holds a deeper meaning for you. Cut it out and place it in the notebook pocket. This is the beginning of a personal inspiration book, or prayer journal. It can reflect the unique busy person that you are. Consider it a long-term project. But begin.

When insights strike you, or a Scripture passage leaps out at you, make a note in this keepsake notebook. And do not judge yourself if Father Time passes you by and the entries are not consistent. You have begun something wonderful. And beginning is enough.

Are you rolling your eyes? Are you thinking: "Starting a prayer journal is just one more thing to add to the list of stuff to do." It's not. Trust me. You will gain amazing insights and experience moments to be cherished. It will give energy to your busy moments. It is encouraging to page through a notebook of consoling moments many months later and rediscover God's presence. Such a prayer notebook comes together bit by bit over time. And when you feel low, this notebook can be a reminder that "this, too, shall pass."

Watch out for that self-censor who tells you not to doodle or wander or leave some lines blank. Go ahead and break all the rules for good grammar if you want. Draw and scribble wherever you wish. This is not going to be graded by anyone. The aim of this notebook is to remind you of beautiful ideas, moments, and inspirations. All of these are prayer.

You can reread the personal prayer notebook to glean new perspective. You can add to it when you feel joy. Perhaps it will help you to delve deeper into a concept that is meaningful on a given day. And when you are really busy, just running past that place where the notebook sits on a table or desk will remind you to turn the current fleeting moment into a prayer. It is not even necessary to pick it up. Sometimes just seeing it resting there is enough to remind you to say, "I love you, Lord." Allow that stationery messenger to call you to a brief "thank you, God, for this breath (or sigh)" and just recognize that God IS in this moment. God is longing for you.

God is thinking of you at every moment, even when we are unaware of that loving gaze focused on us.

You will, of course, have days to lament, and feel free to record those, too. Think about how God might respond to you as you write down your thoughts. Rereading some of those difficult moments can offer you opportunities to glean new insights. It's amazing what you learn by looking back. It's like noticing a glorious sunset in your rear-view mirror as you drive toward a grey and darkening sky.

> *Invite God to bless your work.*

Be free to record whatever you like in the personal prayer journal, and invite God to bless your work. Record reasons to be grateful, and return to these pages months—and even years—later to be uplifted again.

And if you like schedules, you might want to try setting a meeting on your calendar at a specific time every day. Have your prayer notebook handy. This appointment can be considered a very important "conference call" with God, so endeavor to let nothing supplant that appointment. Take that commitment as seriously as you would take an appointment for an annual performance review. Be there!

Can you manufacture time?

Be gentle with yourself as you start to look for moments in your busy life where you can fit in prayer.

People say, "I don't *have* time for that activity," when actually what they mean is "I haven't *made* time for that activity." Choices, sometimes consciously and sometimes reactively, govern how each day moves into memory. Some of the ways in which time evaporates are the result of not paying attention. Rather than complain that I am impacted by my schedule as a passive participant, I need to own up to the fact that I ultimately choose how to spend my finite days. Perhaps one of the first steps to getting started in prayer is to look at some individual choices.

For example, one day my son called me at work and said, "I really need your advice. I am having a crisis." I didn't say, "Gee, sorry. I'm too busy and don't have time. Can you call me tomorrow"? No. I pushed my chair back from my desk, averted my eyes from the documents before me, and focused on an imaginary horizon so that my son was my primary focus. I made time because he is important. And do you know what? I didn't feel bad about giving up something on my "to-do" list to make time for him. I acted out of a personal set of priorities that I choose to live by: family first.

Do you volunteer at the soup kitchen? Watch a movie? Visit a bookstore? Take a nap or play a video game? Prepare a meal for a sick friend? Attend a sporting event? You have the power to choose, even though sometimes people act out of a sense of obligation as if they are powerless to choose.

Our choices can inspire us to greater peace of mind. Think before you choose. Ask yourself what values are driving your decisions. It's worthwhile to do some soul searching and take time to make a list of your priorities in life.

Who obliges you to do various activities? A wise person once told me I did not have to be at every little league game, and that my son's participation must give *him* intrinsic joy. It must not be dependent upon an audience. This concept is anathema to some parents. I discovered my friend was right: I could spend better quality time with my son off the field than the hours we spent with me eating a lukewarm hotdog on the sidelines and him daydreaming in the outfield. I missed a game or two and allowed him to take ownership of his participation and find his own sense of accomplishment in it. My participation in activities should give me intrinsic joy, too.

Once a busy person signs up for a specific group or club membership, it carries with it a sense of obligation, and this sense can rob me of feeling free to structure my time differently. It is worthwhile to step back and evaluate whether some activity feels more like an obligation and a drain than an uplifting activity anticipated with eagerness.

What if your choice to do one thing is a decision to avoid doing something else? Taking time to watch a television rerun may be a choice to avoid cleaning the shower, for example, or washing the car.

> *Figuring out what is influencing the hours of the day takes some careful evaluation.*

We all need down time, and I am not suggesting you give up recreation! What I am proposing is an exercise to help you notice what is happening while you are rushing through your day. Figuring out what is influencing the hours of the day takes some careful evaluation.

My husband finds it very useful in sticking to a diet to record everything he eats in the day. What about recording everything you do in a certain hour, to see if somehow "empty activities" have crept into the schedule? Don't try to do this for every hour; just make an effort to get a better understanding about how your personal commodity of time is spent. Perhaps some new insight will surface.

I feel so much better when I claim my time choices and give myself permission to choose differently from society's expectations. When someone asks me to walk in the annual "Worthwhile-Cause-a-Thon" I can respond lovingly, "I would love to, but I am not able to *make* time for that this year." This keeps the door open for participation at some future point. It also gives a sense of control over the drippy faucet that time can be in our lives. Before we know it, we've filled a bucket to overflowing with lost droplets.

The expression "we have to find the time..." seems impossible to achieve. As if we went on a treasure hunt, we could find bags of time under a tree! To cultivate a relationship with God, through prayer, we have to *make* time, which doesn't sound any easier.

We cannot open a factory and manufacture new units of time. We *can* notice how increments of time slip through our grasp. We can learn to amend unrealistic expectations for ourselves and see more realistically what can be accomplished in a given day. We can become more aware of both our own powerlessness over certain circumstances and our ability to impact even one minute with a positive spin. When time slips away, ask yourself, "Is there something I can learn from this recent drain on my time?" And for heaven's sake do not beat yourself up emotionally if you catch yourself wasting time. Be gentle with your discovery process.

Let us endeavor to choose proactively, and pause when possible to ask quickly, "Lord what would *You* like me to do?"

St. Peter Canisius once said when he was asked if he felt overworked: "If you have too much to do, with God's help you will find time to do it all."

It is also true that God cannot be outdone in generosity, and a few minutes set aside to hear and to speak with God will be rewarded generously somehow by the Creator of time itself. God can make time for us a more meaningful experience and God can manufacture a more peaceful moment out of a frenetic one. *Have you asked God into your moment when you need time most?*

Busy can be crazy

The pages of this book may seem like a crazy quilt. They include several scraps in varying hues—each with a unique character— that are stitched together to create something new. Some appear in a new light based on the influence of the neighboring material. A complicated or complex life is sewn into one whole, thanks to many unrelated experiences brought together. Busy people always seem to be pulling together a multitude of threads.

One of these scraps may be a phone call that interrupts a project of the moment, bringing news of a close friend who shares experiences that are far from one's present routine. Another "color" appears as the radio sounds an alarm with news of a broken world. A framed picture on the wall of the ocean or a mountain scene catches the eye and transcends the present time and place.

Each busy life is unique and more beautiful because of the scraps that come together. May the solutions you seek lead you to a deeper sense of how God pulls all the disjointed pieces into something that isn't crazy at all. God adds "filler" and provides the foundation for the whole of life – a seamless fabric behind it all. Don't forget that the church and your community contribute to the patchwork. Invite others to celebrate and know your story. You are a sacramental life: a visible sign of God's active presence in the world.

As must be done in gardening, you may be drawn to prune away some habits or practices of your life. And some of the passages in this book won't fit. Don't force things. Other concepts will blossom as you consider them. Stay with what produces results. A feeling of peace is a sure sign of God at work.

> *Stay with what produces results.*

Sometimes when I sit down to pray, it can feel a little like weeding. ("When do I get to the fun part? I think I would rather put this off. When will I see results?")

Keep trying, be persistent, and don't judge yourself. Follow what brings peace. An agitated heart is not what God hopes for in us. God's plan is for peace amidst the storms of schedules.

Take time to look at the core assumptions you are making not only about prayer and what it is, but also about God, who God is, and how God can reach out to you. Get to know your own prayer style. For some it's meditation (for some, this feels like torture). For some, it's music, or dance (for some this feels awkward or artificial). Some love studying scripture. Some love rote prayer. Tell yourself that one prayer style is not better than another. Start breaking the rules you hold for prayer. Prayer doesn't happen only if I sit quietly, or go to church.

Believe it or not, God is always looking for you, whether or not you are looking for God. Don't be afraid to reflect on your busy life, and start looking for those places and times where God is interrupting you, or alongside you. God invites you to notice the presence of true Love amidst the chaos of today.

Then pick up your prayer journal and jot down one small thought about your hope for this busy day.

Chapter 2

A moment on eating: Food for thought

Feeling too busy seems to be the normal condition for everyone in today's society. Our culture seems to make it impossible for us to live any other way. We have obligations and occupations. We have myriad choices for entertainments and activities, plus desires that pull us in all directions. We have so many *good* options that we can feel *less good* by the end of a day, when one too many good things happened.

This book is not a manual on how *not* to be busy. Perhaps a side benefit of following some of the tips in these pages will be a less busy lifestyle. But this book is not a cure for the crazed. A cure does not exist. People in this century are going to encounter plenty of temptations to be over-busy.

Within such lives, however, we can stay with or get connected with the God who loves us and who will find us no matter where we work, play, serve, and yes, hide.

Prayer and growing in relationship with the Almighty are like food. None of us eats only once a week and remains healthy. Many of us do take shortcuts in nutrition, but we know we feel ill or overtired when we skip eating altogether. The latest research reveals that better health is achieved by eating at least five smaller meals in a day. Perhaps prayer can be viewed in the same way, especially for busy people: we need frequent nibbles.

If you, like most busy people, are feeling overtired, spiritually overdrawn, or just plain cranky (and others will notice when you've consumed the last of your loving energies. Hopefully they will notify you), then it's time for some spiritual food. Let's take this analogy further.

A brief prayer can be like a meal on the run. To what could we compare a coffee break? It could take the form of some spiritually uplifting reading that you find on the Internet, or a page from an inspiring book (remember, you don't have to read every book start to finish, or in order).

Of course, we all enjoy the opportunity to devote time to a leisurely meal. On occasion, we can spend a significant amount of time with beloved friends sipping cocktails and munching some hors d'oeuvres, and perusing a menu at length. Soon we are telling the waitress we need a little more time, and then we are waiting without concern for the appearance of the first course. We relax over every serving of the meal, enjoying the spaces between courses. Perhaps a bottle of wine or two makes an appearance, and by the time dessert rolls around, we feel relaxed and unconcerned that the better part of an evening is past. We may even be the last people in the restaurant by this time. And the memories of the evening and the relaxed atmosphere remain with us for a long, long time.

Perhaps the prayerful equivalent of this is a weekend retreat. We leave "the mountain top" refreshed and more at peace than when we began. Perhaps others see the difference immediately. When God is at work, the effects are longlasting, and others benefit.

Such sumptuous banquets are to be treasured. But between these special occasions, we still have to eat!

So for this moment, consider how you eat, both physically and prayerfully. Just think about your current habits. Do you skip breakfast? Eat in your car? Enjoy a coffee break? Go out for

lunch? Pack a snack? Eat leftovers? Imbibe too many treats?
Prepare meals for others? Take vitamins? Share meals at
someone else's home?

And do you say a rote prayer
before meals? Pray for whoever is in that
ambulance when you hear a siren? Say
thanks to God right out of the blue?

Think about parallels in your
prayer time to some of the different ways
you eat. Perhaps in the margin you can
list some ideas.

The goal is to widen your
perspective on what constitutes prayer,
and to become more aware of the times in
your life when you are already at prayer
or times where you can easily add a little
morsel of prayer to the moment.

It is also possible to associate the
act of physically eating with the actions of
prayer. Some of us already have a habit of
grace before meals. Can we expand it by a sentence? Be more
aware of the words and their meaning? Add in a phrase for those
who have nothing?

Busy people may find that expressing gratitude for
everything we eat may lead to a deepening awareness of God in
the ordinary circumstances of each day.

Where and with whom do you worship? When do you feel
spiritually fed? Have you been surprised by the places where
you notice God? God may be feeding you snacks all day long.
How often is your prayer asking God for assistance of one kind
or another? How often do you give thanks?

> *The goal is to widen your perspective on what constitutes prayer, and to become more aware of the times in your life when you are already at prayer. Where can I easily add a little morsel of fleeting prayer to the moment?*

Next, consider two clichés: "What's eating you?" and "You are what you eat." How do our minds chew on ideas, perceptions, assumptions, and problems? How do intangibles consume us?

The answers to these questions may stimulate a prayerful response. Here are some suggestions to get you started:

- *"Lord, please help me understand the connections between how I treat others and what I feed my mind and what I feed my heart."*
- *"Lord, I want to be aware of how I eat 'the daily bread' you give."*
- *"Thank you for the food you provide for me."*
- *"Develop in me a deeper sense of gratitude."*
- *"Jesus, I feel stuffed!"*
- *"Jesus, I'm starving!"*
- *"Father, will you offer me a tiny morsel of inspiration in this moment?"*

Christ certainly spent a great deal of time eating, as we see in the Gospels. He moves from one meal to another, whether in Cana, or at a tax collector's house, or at Simon's mother-in-law's or elsewhere. It is no accident that the most intimate gesture of our Catholic faith is a meal: consuming the body and blood of Christ in the Eucharist.

Busy people are often involved in decision making, leading, and carrying burdens for others. The Eucharist is an opportunity to receive, and let God lead. The ritual offers comfort, and the food of the Eucharist is unbeatable nourishment for the busy soul.

Food is important. And it's not optional. You need to eat to stay alive. If you want to be spiritually fit, you better spiritually eat. You have to pray to keep your soul healthy. And not every meal will be a gourmet feast. But real nourishment can be found in tidbits and snacks.

And don't forget supplements. An engineer who regularly makes time for weekday Mass taught me about taking spiritual vitamins. These are short lines from Scripture that offer encouragement and consolation. If you are feeling out of sorts, ask yourself what supplements you have been putting into your daily prayer diet.

He advocates memorizing a few Biblical inspirations. Do you have some favorites already? Repeat them several times a day to fortify yourself in the busyness of your life.

Here are a few suggestions:

- *"For God did not give us a spirit of fear but of power and love, and a sound mind, with understanding."* *2 Timothy 1:6-8*
- *"The Lord is my help. I will not be afraid. What can anyone do to me?"* *Hebrews 13: 5-6*
- *I have strength for everything through Christ who empowers me." Philippians 4:13*
- *"The Lord is my shepherd. I shall not want." Psalm 23:1*

Take a spiritual vitamin.
It's worth the time you take to memorize an inspirational line. It will return to you when you need it most. Start slow, with a goal that is realistic for you.

The Scriptures are full of food imagery. Chew on some of these:

- *"My soul shall be filled as with choice food." Psalm 63:5*
- *"You spread a table before me in the sight of my foes..."* *Psalm 23*

- *"He sent an abundance of food..." Psalm 78:24-30*
- *"I am the bread of life." John 6:35*
- *"The one who feeds on me will have life because of me." John 6:57*
- *What Father would give his children stones when they ask for food?" Matthew 7:9*

Remember Joseph, who during a time of famine fed Egypt from the stores of grain during lean years? It was hunger that reunited separated brothers and led to reconciliation (Genesis 41:53-47:11). The brothers come to Egypt begging for bread, which leads to the next step in God's plan for God's people: life in Egypt, the Passover, and eating the lamb, a ritual celebrated to this day and transformed into something new by Christ at the Last Supper.

Many hymns celebrate our connection with food. For example, *"Bread of Heaven, feed me till I want no more"* (Peter Williams), and *"You satisfy the hungry heart with gift of finest wheat"* (Robert Kreutz and Omer Westendorf).

> *Ask God to feed you and to help you establish a pattern of regular, daily time for prayer.*

One other suggestion is to begin to pray the Our Father every morning, lingering over the words in your mind, "Give us this day our daily bread." Ask God to feed you and to help you establish a pattern of regular, daily time for prayer.

How much is enough? That will depend upon where you are in your relationship with God right now. For some people, adding an Our Father every day is a big step and a new habit to cultivate. Such a new routine is a marvelous enterprise. It is great to take that step! Other people spend half an hour at prayer every morning, and check in for a moment halfway through the day, and then have a routine for a few minutes of prayer before bedtime. What would be too much for one person would be just enough for another.

I know a woman who owns a giant hourglass similar to the one the wicked witch used in "The Wizard of Oz." This woman uses the timepiece to remain faithful to a commitment of one hour of prayer early every morning. And yes, she is a very busy person the other 23 hours of her day. Her high-pressure job, her service to the homeless, and her care for her family are enlivened by her commitment to prayer.

Taking time out for prayer fits into the category of rest. And rest is something American society devalues and even sacrifices in favor of accomplishment and production.

Do you think God made the third commandment, to take a day of Sabbath rest, for himself? I don't think so. God created the human body with a basic need, as basic as food, for rest and relaxation.

Take a look at Hebrews 4:9-11. "A Sabbath rest still remains for the people of God" and "Strive to enter into that rest."

Put prayer into the category of Sabbath rest for yourself. Build it into your diet. It is just as necessary for living.

Prayer is not something that only occurs during formal periods. Actions, too, are prayer. The next chapters provide some further food for thought on how to discover ways you already pray during your busy life.

Chapter 3

Moments of action:

A new way of thinking about a busy day

How can they ask me to do one more thing?

"While you are at the bank, can you stop at the post office and send this package?"

With a smile or a sigh, I comply. And in that moment's choice, to react with joy — "I would be happy to help" — or with frustration —"*Not* one more thing to do!" — is the secret to whether "too busy" takes over.

Remember the words of the 23rd psalm: "The Lord is my shepherd. There is nothing I lack." You lack nothing, including enough time.

God knows how much time you have, and gives you enough. Do you *really* think the Lord of all time can't give you enough, or isn't giving you enough? If so, then ask the Lord about it. Talk to God about your desire for more.

I can safely *add* a kind act, a gentle word, a momentary service, and actually *subtract* from the disquiet that eats at my hurried heart. Am I really too busy, or am I too focused on myself and my story? Perhaps by making a choice to perform a loving act, I change perspective and transform my day with a new attitude.

It is valuable to examine one's expectations. Do you expect to do only the things you want to do or that you prioritize as important? To control your own life? Some of us expect to make everyone around us happy and attempt to do this at the expense of our own peace. Do you expect to live forever? At the root of many frustrations for busy people is a set of unrealistic expectations of what is humanly possible to accomplish in a fixed, finite time.

Yes, we are frail, and given little time, the book of Wisdom tells us. [2]

Still, the time is enough according to God's clock for us. The secret to being less busy, perhaps, is downsizing our expectations for ourselves and for others. Am I expecting too much of me? Not enough of God's miraculous power and love?

I review my expectations. What did these expectations bring about for me today? What feelings arose out of what I wanted to accomplish?

I amend my expectations for tomorrow, and I reflect on the notion that doing less allows me to enjoy more.

Or God may be inviting me to let some things go. I know I make myself anxious about many things which may be better left alone. I forget to pray before I act.

God will meet you wherever you are. Invite God into your busy day.

Prayer in action

The old cliché, "actions speak louder than words," can be insightful when you look at your prayer life. An errand can steal

---

[2] Wisdom 9:5.

your smile, or it can give you a fresh one if the errand is approached as a new way to serve someone in need.

Isn't helping those in need what Christ is all about? He healed and washed feet and gave many examples of "working overtime." Like the day he was at a party in Cana and he was pressed into service to create wine at the request of a concerned third party—his mom.

> *Do you think of activity as prayer? More than likely, you are immersed in a life of prayer already due to the actions you perform selflessly for others.*

Take a moment to examine the activities of yesterday to see whom you may have helped, heard, or held in the regular processes of your day. To paraphrase Mother Teresa, some of the greatest poverty in the world is among people who have plenty of material possessions.[3] So when you help a customer at work or ignore the driver who cuts you off on the freeway, consider it a service to Christ. When you see Christ in the other person, this is prayer in action.

Do you think of activity as prayer? More than likely, you are immersed in a life of prayer already due to the actions you perform selflessly for others.

The first letter to the Thessalonians (5:17) suggests that we should "pray without ceasing." If this is true, then there must be a way to transform the ordinary tasks of our day into prayer.

---

[3] "The spiritual poverty of the Western World is much greater than the physical poverty of our people," she told Dan Wooding in 1975 (ASSIST News Service, July 4, 2010. See www.assistnews.com). On another occasion, she said, "We think sometimes that poverty is only being hungry, naked and homeless. The poverty of being unwanted, unloved or uncared for is the greatest poverty. We must start in our own homes to remedy this kind of poverty."

Remember: prayer is growing the relationship we enjoy with God. And sometimes that relationship grows by serving.

In *The Call to Discernment in Troubled Times*, Dean Brackley explains that actions deepen our relationship with God. Brackley says that according to St. Ignatius of Loyola, "If we are seeking to do God's will, we are no less united to God in *busy confusion* (emphasis added) than in formal prayer. We need be no less united to God washing the dishes than when at the Eucharist. If possible, we should find no less devotion in driving the school bus than in prayer." [4]

This concept gives me hope. Cleaning the coffee pot at work, even when I didn't drink any coffee today, becomes an imitation of Christ serving at the last supper.

It would be a mistake to suppose that silent times and formal periods of prayer are unnecessary because a person's actions are sufficient by themselves. At the same time, we must not assume that people aren't praying because they live a busy life. Balance is a key.

How does one arrive at a position of completing activities in ways that make them prayers? What alters something from being a grudgingly done favor to being an act of kindness? The answer to this question will be different for different people.

My mother was a strong proponent of the Apostleship of Prayer.[5] These folks dedicate themselves to a "Morning Offering," which makes each and every movement and idea in

---

[4] Dean Brackley, *The Call to Discernment in Troubled Times: New Perspectives on the Transformative Wisdom of Ignatius Loyola* (New York: Crossroad, 2004), p. 246. All of chapter 26 is an excellent guide for busy people. I highly recommend this book.

[5] It is estimated that 50 million people worldwide claim membership to this Apostleship of Prayer, which began in 1844 in France. For more information, see www.apostleshipofprayer.org/.

the day into a prayer. I think St. Paul would approve. Here is their traditional morning offering:

> *"Dear Jesus, through the immaculate heart of*
> *Mary, I offer you my prayers, work, joys and*
> *sufferings of this day, in union with the holy*
> *sacrifice of the Mass throughout the world. I*
> *offer them for all the intentions of your Sacred*
> *Heart: the salvation of souls, reparation for sin,*
> *and the reunion of all Christians. I offer them*
> *for all the intentions of our bishops, and all*
> *members of the Apostleship of Prayer, and in*
> *particular, those intentions recommended by*
> *our Holy Father for this month."*

My dad taught us as children a much shorter version that maintains the intent. This prayer is a bit easier for a busy person to squeeze in:

> *"Good morning, dear Jesus. This day is for you.*
>
> *I ask you to bless all I think, say, and do."*

Now, I even switch this prayer up a bit (which makes it less poetic) so that the second line goes like this:

> *May all I think, say, and do be as*
> *you'd want me to.*

Since I am usually on the go, memorized prayers help me take prayer along on the run.

> *Dedicating to God ahead of time every possible potential occurrence of the day opens new paths.*

Other busy people confirm that having something committed to memory facilitates prayer "on the go." Memorizing a morning offering can transform the days into praise. Everything is dedicated to the One who first dedicated the Son to us.

God longs for us to be aware of the Holy Presence constantly with us. New paths open when we dedicate to God ahead of time every possible potential occurrence of the day. It may seem odd at first, but try it! As new activities start, you may discover a more peaceful approach to situations. You may encounter people in new ways, knowing that this action is taking place with God tagging along. Even when we forget, God's loving gaze is still looking at us.

Most Christians share the conviction that we are to imitate Christ. Busy people will benefit from remembering that Jesus really enjoyed his life. He loved being alive. He had friends and he spent time serving people. We share the same call to enjoy our ordinary moments in life. Don't allow the feeling that you are too busy rob you of enjoying each day.

In that enjoyment of life, chances are that you are a grace to someone today and that you were a blessing to someone yesterday, too. Maybe you were not even aware of it, but it is still true. God works through you even when you are not paying attention.

To whom will you be a grace today?

Now just a minute!

If only the things we say will "only take a minute" really did! How many times do people tell me to "wait a minute" or that they will put me on hold for just a minute?

So I tried it: I sat in silence doing nothing but watching a clock measuring 60 seconds. I took off my watch and held it over three fingers on each hand, uniting my fingertips to lock me out of doing something. It was very difficult to sit still for that minute, knowing I had my busy list waiting.

On another occasion, I witnessed a minute pass on an enormous clock face, the kind often found in a grade school classroom. It seems the larger the clock, the longer the second hand, and the longer it seems to take to traverse one rotation. Lord! I thought that minute would never end so I could get back to my agenda!

Am I enjoying the minutes I spend on my busy list of things to accomplish?

How many minutes do I get in a day, really?

Grab a half minute here. Reclaim half a minute there. And evaluate your feelings, thoughts, and the recurring assumptions that are lying just below the surface of your consciousness. What assumptions do you make about prayer? Does it have to take an hour? Can it take just a few seconds?

For one minute listen to your inhalations and exhalations. You can either empty your thoughts, or invite God to reveal something to you. A newly married young man, who meditates for perhaps half an hour every day, finds that creating space for silence is a critical part of his wellbeing. It centers him for the other parts of the day. And he spends less time straightening out arguments with his wife over his bad temper.

> *What will you try to do the next time you are asked to wait a minute?*

Beginners may find that after 30 seconds, they are anxious to get up and get moving. But stick it out. Will you be different or feel different after you take a moment to evaluate one minute? Unfortunately, this is not guaranteed to immediately lift your mind to a higher realm. There are no magic formulas. But in faith, you can believe that a minute given to God is never wasted.

What will you try to do the next time you are asked to wait a minute? Might you let those words be a signal to trigger a momentary pause? When you hear, "can you wait just a minute?" try seeing it as a call to prayer. Imagine a bell ringing out an invitation. This will take some practice. Perhaps you will then be able to enjoy the wait.

As a James Taylor lyric says, "The secret of life is enjoying the passage of time."

Habit forming

"Whatever you *do*, in word or action, *do* everything in the name of the Lord Jesus, giving thanks to God the Father through Christ" (Col. 3:17).

> *Prayer in action can become a habit.*

Your moments of action are ways you give of yourself. If you can form a habit of measuring your actions against the yardstick of love, over time your activities will grow in conformity to God's way of doing things. Remember another recommendation from St. Paul in 1Corinthians 16:14: Your every act should be done with love.

God is love and cannot be outdone in generosity. Your actions during an active day may be interrupted by a person you can serve as if it were Christ. I pray you will encounter a sense of God's presence appearing within your consciousness as you go about your busy day. You are not alone. God chooses to join us in our humble lives and is truly present in our hearts. Prayer in action can become a habit.

Chapter 4

Wait a minute!

Questions to ponder

Busy people don't always take time to ask themselves some deeper questions.

Is it possible for me to slow down?
What would I have to give up to do so?

Do I do things because "if I don't do it, no one else will"? Is it pride that compels me to take on too much because I think I am the only one who will do it "right"?

Do I allow myself to become a victim by saying yes? Am I behaving in a codependent manner?

Am I busy because I like it? Because I want to be? Because it makes me feel needed, useful, important or wanted? Was I raised to be busy?

Has society or culture led me to a busy life, and I never really noticed that I keep getting busier and busier?

Do I fill my life with noise and activity because I am afraid of quiet? Afraid of what I might hear?

Am I afraid to see some aspect of my life in clear view? Am I trying to avoid looking at places where I need to forgive and heal?

If I stop being so busy, what will I have to change in myself?

Am I busy because I said yes too many times without thought or intentionally choosing?

If my energy has waned and I'm feeling angry or misused, is it because I wasn't selective in what I agreed to do? Was I afraid to say no?

If you can, clear some time on your calendar to dare to be silent, and ponder a question that most irritates you.

Ask God one of these questions and listen to see if God responds. See if a new insight comes to you, and thank God for it.

Prayer is how God and I get to know each other.

Perhaps this time of intentional listening will lead you to more questions.

Difficult questions

Do I run from darkness? Fear suffering? Wish for simple solutions? Hide behind achievements? What wakes me up at night? What do I fear most?

In her book, *Inner Compass*, Margaret Silf explains that our "deepest desire has a reverse face, where our deepest fear is imprinted."[6] If I am brave enough to identify the things I fear most (for example, going unnoticed), I can discover my deepest motivations (longing for significance, of being important to someone). When my deepest wishes are no longer a secret to myself, I can understand better why I am making the choices I make in my life.

---

[6] Margaret Silf, *Inner Compass* (Chicago: Loyola Press, 1999), p. 72.

Am I doing many activities to run from the big thing I should be doing? Am I allowing clutter and noise to detract and distract from discernment, to distract me from my path—the way God hopes I will take?

Am I achieving some good thing as a way of putting off doing some greater good to which God is calling me?

Am I using my busy schedule to run from God's voice and call? What am I running from?

Is the life I am now living the life God wants for me?

Have I asked God to lead me to that life?

Use the space below to write down your own questions. Or record them in your journal. Don't rush to answer.

Ponder, as would Mary, the Mother of God and great holder of thoughts in her heart (see Luke 2:19).

Chapter 5

Awareness: Wake up and smell the coffee

At Starbucks, a man sits with a newspaper, engrossed in a news article. He is aware of little else. Suddenly a crash awakens him to the broken coffee mug nearby and he helps retrieve pieces for the teen at the next table. He smiles and returns to his reading. A beautiful woman striding into line calls his awareness away once more.

What do you notice? What triggers you to be aware of something outside yourself? Each morning, we take a moment to look into a mirror. It may be while shaving, tying a tie, brushing teeth or hair, or giving one's outfit a last once-over before heading out the door. During the course of the day, you may forget to be aware of how you look. Your physical appearance does not cease to exist simply because it is outside your conscious awareness. You may find your physical appearance returning to your mind when an attractive member of the opposite sex happens by.

> *What triggers you to be aware of something outside yourself?*

How can a busy person be more aware of God? How do we grow in awareness that every moment can be a prayer? What awakens your senses that God is present?

Busy people can incorporate a wide range of triggers into their day to call to mind the reality that God is always present. Things that are already taking place may be used to awaken a moment of prayerful presence.

Prayer in the shower

Who doesn't like to take a nice, long, hot shower? Yes! You can pray in your bathroom! As you start your shower, recall the waters of baptism. Allow yourself to remember as if you are being baptized again in the shower. Then, as you wash, consecrate your body to the work God knows you will do this day. Offer this corporal self to the service of God. As you wash your own feet, ask God to bless your steps: "Let each step I take, oh Lord, be in service to you."

As you wash your hands, ask God to help these hands be a blessing to someone today. Let the shower water cleanse you spiritually of yesterday's mistakes, shortcomings, and omissions. Prepare your body as a holy offering to God.

As you towel yourself dry, be open to the notion that God may use your bathroom to speak to you! It may be the only quiet moment you get today, if you are headed to a hectic schedule. Treasure the gift of this moment of preparing to meet a new day.

Mentally put on a white garment if you don't happen to be dressing in something white today, and remember that you are forgiven. A new day begins. Receive the light of Christ. Start fresh.

Make a note of that

If you are a listmaker, crossing off accomplishments as you go, consider making a new type of list. As fast as you can, list 25 things that cause you to give thanks. Count them off. This is a good way to develop a habit of gratitude. For example: "I opened my eyes to a new day. 1) Thank you, God, I can see. 2) Thank you for colors. 3) Thank you for the fact that I can put two feet on the ground as I get out of bed." You get the idea.

Some of us are fond of making notes. Perhaps you can leave yourself an inspirational quote on that note. Or draw a small cross, just to remind you of Christ's love shown on the cross. Your note can bring to your awareness God's self-giving love.

Consider what visual reminders you have in your immediate environment that call your favorite people to mind. A photo in your wallet? A keychain someone gave you? A vase of flowers? A knickknack on your desk? Pictures on the refrigerator?

Consider adding a reminder of God to your daily routine.

Someone gave me a key chain with a religious symbol on it. Over time, I have forgotten to notice it, but it is still there, and occasionally I see it. (I wonder if others notice it even when I don't, like the valet parking lot attendant downtown.)

> *What reminders of God are easily available in your daily routines?*

That key chain gave me an idea. I put a miraculous medal into the change compartment of my wallet. Many times, I am surprised to find it there when I dump the change into my hand. A half sentence of gratitude to God passes in the cathedral of my heart as I thank the cashier aloud for ringing up my groceries and I return the unused change and the medal to the zipped compartment. Did the cashier notice the medal? Did it call forth a remembrance of God from him also? I will never know.

What's in your glove box? Your bedside table? Even your silverware drawer? What if you added a card with an uplifting thought or Scripture reference to one of these places? I can't tell you how often this practice reminds me to pray when I surprise myself with a quote or word that I put there weeks before. I find a momentary boost of love. And that note in the silverware drawer surprises guests to my home, too, and perhaps invites them to take a fleeting moment to thank God.

Take it to heart

In Deuteronomy 6:6-8, we read, "Take to heart these words I enjoin on you today."[7]

How do we take God's words to heart? The verse continues: "bind them at your wrist as a sign and let them be as a pendant on your forehead. Write them on the doorposts of your houses and on your gates." Not a bad idea, really, to place visual reminders in every room in our homes to remind us of what is most important in our lives. Can you add a Scripture quote or a picture from a beautiful Christmas card to your refrigerator door?

Colorful rubber bracelets are popular cause-promoters. Ask someone why they wear a specific bracelet and you will hear everything from support for cancer research and solidarity with people in recovery to care for a person with epilepsy and awareness of diabetes. Are you willing to sport a medal, a rosary bracelet, a crucifix, or some article of clothing that reminds you and others to pray during a busy day?

Images mean a lot to us, and a simple crucifix, Scripture quote or photograph on display can be subtle calls to us: "The Lord is our God. Love with your whole heart." It doesn't have to be large, and it doesn't have to be obvious, especially if you need

---

[7] Deuteronomy 6:6 comes immediately after the Shema, the centerpiece of Jewish morning and evening prayer: "Hear, O Israel! The Lord is our God, the Lord alone! Therefore, you shall love the Lord, your God, with all your heart, and with all your soul, and with all your strength."

to pay special attention to workplace regulations. Perhaps you keep it under your keyboard, where only you stumble upon it from time to time.

Here's another idea: find yourself a clip that will attach to your car visor if you don't have one there already for some other purpose. Then take a favorite saying from the Bible or a small picture such as a holy card or icon that gives you inspiration, and attach it to the clip. When the visor is up, that image is waiting to be discovered.

I find that this visual reminder not only invites me to a quick prayer now and then, but also it is a sign to others who join me in my car that someone who loves God drives this vehicle. It is a small way to be a witness to the Christian life. My car becomes a sanctuary. When I feel self-conscious about this little visual, I ask God for the courage to admit my faith in public.

> *This visual reminder not only invites me to a quick prayer now and then, but also it is a sign to others.*

We can also create reminders beyond visual ones.

A smart phone allows you to keep your calendar, contacts, and even the World Wide Web in the palm of your hand. It also allows you to set a daily, repeating alarm as a reminder to do something. I use this cool feature to set an appointment at 1:11 every day. When the alarm goes off, I am reminded to review what has happened in my day thus far, and to thank God who has brought me to this current moment. If I have forgotten to check in with God, the alarm provides a gentle reminder.

Such a reminder to pray makes your everyday phone an instrument of prayer. And yes, it goes off at inconvenient times, too. It just may give you an opportunity to witness to your faith, if you are brave enough, to explain why this alarm is causing you to pause. Perhaps you will invite people to join you in a silent moment when the alarm strikes. Through that invitation, you will perform an act of service and even evangelization. How easy it can be to affect a life beyond our own.

How can I follow the call in the closing phrases of Mark's Gospel to evangelize? Perhaps I am called to simple awarenesses, and to let God open doors for me to explain to others the reason for my hope (1 Peter 3:15).

I once gave my sister the gift of a daily prayer for a year. I lifted up her needs daily when that soft-toned alarm rang on my smartphone.

What to do next

As any day unfolds, we have many occasions to transition to new activities. Occasionally, we have big decisions to make. Journaling is one way to discern the next step or the next activity we seek to undertake.

Is it a "shake the dust" and "let that activity go" moment, or is it a "take up your cross and follow me" moment when the best choice is to press on? Is it a "Father, into your hands I commit myself" moment where a written reflection helps sort out our attitudes? Writing can awaken awareness.

Sometimes it is in the rambling sentences written on a page that the best choice to make becomes apparent or takes shape. Rereading what you have written a few days from now may give the insight you desire when trying to make a decision about taking on a new responsibility. Sometimes busy people just jump in and say, "Sure! I'll do it," rather than reflect on whether they are the best person to do this or not. It is okay to ask people to wait a day for your decision. When someone asks you to take on a new task it could be a trigger for you to spend a few seconds, or more, in prayer.

One technique to try is to ask yourself questions in written form, in your journal, and allow yourself to write yourself an answer.

Sometimes just forming a question adds to your clarity of mind. Think about what graces, or gifts, you need from God right now. What is it you would like to ask God to give? Is it patience, perseverance, balance, or relief?

As you try to answer the questions as you imagine God would, watch what words come to your pen. See if anything new surfaces in your subconscious. I am often surprised by the sentences that flow.

Another tool I use in my prayer notebook is to slowly, deliberately, draw a large empty square. Nothing is to be written in there. You are holding the space open. Available. It is an image of the space we want to make where God's still, quiet voice can be heard.

... holding space open.

Establishing new patterns for prayer

My mother, who loved crafts, gave me one of the "prayer rocks" she was assembling for a church bazaar. She was putting one-inch stones on a swatch of fabric and securing the stone inside with lovely ribbons. She added a note to each that instructed the owner to place the rock on your pillow at night so you would clunk your head on it before going to sleep. It would remind you to pray before bedtime, at which time you were instructed to drop it on the floor, so that you could stub your toe on it in the morning upon awakening, and once again be reminded to pray.

Silly that we need concrete reminders to turn to moments of prayer. But they sure help!

Those of us who have tried to establish daily patterns of prayer know it is not easy. If it triggers my memory to pray, then a rock on my pillow is worth a try!

While I am talking about my mother, who was a woman of great faith, let me describe her homemade prayer companion that she created in her waning years. She kept it by her sewing chair, where she read her morning paper. It was smaller than a sheet of paper folded twice and was no more than eight pages long. She took card stock and glued onto it favorite prayers she ran across. Some were holy cards, and others had come in the mail with some appeal for donations. She glued a picture of the Mother of Perpetual Help icon to the cover. I remember catching her squeezing in a few moments in the morning with that simple booklet. The little guide was the first part of her daily routine in later life. When she died, her executor, my brother, made copies for all of us siblings. While the contents were her favorites and not mine, the booklet is something holy to hold. It motivates me to seek my own stolen moments at prayer.

Think about creating your own small prayer booklet, using passages or quotes that hold great meaning for you. Nothing big. Just something to leaf through occasionally for inspiration or motivation.

"If I could just remember..."

My grandparents, born in Slovakia, had the habit of saying "the body and blood of Christ" each time they entered a home— their own or someone else's. Whoever was home responded, "Forever and ever, Amen." I learned this phrase in Slovak as a child. I don't know why I dropped the habit once I moved out. Growing up in a household with such a greeting, it was easy to remember to offer a quick prayer with each visitor.

I recognize a similar practice in Judaism with the mezuzah. A tiny scroll in a case is affixed to the doorpost of a home's entrance. The scroll inside contains a quote from the book of Deuteronomy: "Hear, oh Israel! The Lord your God is One. And thou shalt love the Lord thy God with all thy heart, and with all thy soul, and with all thy might." People touch the mezuzah when they come and go through the door.

Each of us probably has simple techniques to help us remember important stuff. A note on the dashboard reminds me to buy gas. Leaving a suit in the doorway reminds me to stop at the dry cleaner.

What memory tricks can you think up to help you "wake up" and remember to pray?

A toothbrush?

For one busy woman, it's her toothbrush. She told me that every time she brushes her teeth, she becomes aware that she is face to face with God. "In the morning, I ask, 'What are we going to do today?' You know my list." Then, in the evening, when she looks in the mirror, she says to God, "We did a pretty good job today, didn't we?" Here is a woman who embraces the truth that she is an image of the Most High God, a temple of God's Holy Spirit. And a toothbrush is the memory trick that brings her to prayer.

I am not talking about adding to your daily routine so that you are spending long hours at prayer. We can use existing memory boosters to remind us to grab that brief moment to be mindful of our infinitely loving God.

When you know you are going to be doing something all the time, every day, find a way to incorporate prayer into that action. For example, we all eat meals, and we eat three times a day or more. Some of us have a habit of saying grace before meals. Build on that. If you don't have the habit, cultivate it. Listen to how you say grace and resolve to take this prayer break a little more seriously than a rote repetition. A man I know says, "Eternal rest, grant unto them, oh Lord," after grace, taking a moment to advocate for the souls of departed ancestors, acquaintances, and those who have no one to pray for them.

It is also easy to add to our regular grace before meals a simple prayer such as one of these:

Immaculate Heart of Mary,
pray for us now and at the hour
of our death. Amen.

Or

Bless all who are hungry today.
Bless the hands that brought
these foods to market.

If you are in this before-meal habit of saying grace already, see if you can remember to add a prayer of thanksgiving at the end of your meal, too. A short sentence of gratitude will bless you over time with the fruits of God's peaceful presence in your life.

If you take the garbage out every week, use the walk through the house to ask God to remove the garbage of small sins that accumulated in your behavior all week. The careless words or unkind remarks may seem inconsequential and easily dismissed, but they leave a residue of garbage that God can help us remove. When you take the garbage to the street, say a prayer that every house on your block will also be able to let go of the hurts inevitably inflicted upon one another during the normal course of living with other people.

If you wash the car every Saturday, use a moment to ask God to clean away the grime that separates peoples through unresolved guilt or shame, racism, or societal sins.

And why are we so stingy with making the Sign of the Cross? A simple, wordless blessing of yourself as you hop into a car or cross a threshold into some building acts as a reminder of what your life is really all about. Let go of the fear that someone may see you and think you strange.

Sometimes at the end of a workday, I call my voice mail or send myself an email to the work address with an uplifting thought to begin the next day. Being terribly busy, by the following day, I have forgotten I did this. It's a fun way to surprise myself this way!

Routine. Learn to use it to accommodate your prayer. Where in your ordinary routine can you establish a simple new habit of prayer?

> *Where in your ordinary routine can you establish a simple new habit of prayer?*

What am I praying about?

As you incorporate new tidbits of prayer in your life, look at the content of the prayer. *How*, exactly, do you pray? Are you always asking for something, for example?

You may already be familiar with a memory aid that reminds us of the types of prayer: ACTS. It stands for adoration, contrition, thanksgiving, and supplication. Many of us busy people spend much of our time in supplication and intercession: "Dear God, help me survive this latest crisis!" and its companion,

"Dear God, help my friend/neighbor/relative survive their latest crisis!"

It is fruitful to stop once in a while and ask yourself if your prayers are tipped into one of these important reasons for prayer more than another. Saying we are sorry is not the easiest thing to do, for example. Contrition may not be a daily habit, even though each of us errs regularly somewhere by failing to love fully.

And do I take blessings for granted! It contributes to a frazzled attitude when I do. I behave as if I deserve smooth sailing through life.

Prayers of gratitude are among God's favorites. God loves to be appreciated, and adored. Too often, idols of personal comfort or money get in my way.

When you take a moment to be aware of your prayer life, ask yourself if you are remembering to build your relationship with God in all four of these areas of prayer.

Becoming more aware

If you enjoy coffee each day, consider that Jesus said, "Come to ME all who are thirsty." As you sip that cup—or enjoy some other beverage—remember as the liquid slides down your throat to thank God for quenching your thirst for a closer relationship with the Almighty. Ask for the grace to make it through this day.

Picture God filling you with love, joy, and peace as that beverage quenches your human thirst. Smile! You are praying. In fact, prayer is right under your nose.

Chapter 6

"What am I doing here?"

Evaluating ordinary moments

I often find myself reacting throughout my day, sometimes as if on autopilot, and a day is half spent before I realize that so many small choices occurred. That is why it is so important to step back for a moment and look at where I may have been.

I once was driving in southern Washington, looking ahead at an increasingly gray sky. I glanced in my rearview mirror and almost drove off the road because behind me was a fiery orange sunset with such beauty I gasped aloud. I would have missed it completely had I not looked back.

The same is absolutely true in prayer. We will miss so much beauty if we never reflect back on what happened in our quiet prayer time and during our day, which holds moments when we encountered God. Some moments in the day we only survived because God carried us through. We don't always see this in the midst of the hectic moments, and that is why reflecting back is critical. It opens opportunities to say, "thank you, God!" We become more grateful. Gratitude leads to happier selves. It is in looking back that we will often see the fingerprints of God.

When I was in college, majoring in public relations, we learned that the evaluation step of media campaigns was essential to our success. And performance evaluations at work are common.

Evaluating prayer is simply reviewing the circumstances surrounding prayer to see what surfaced and discovering where the most meaningful insights are. God is present in many of the ordinary moments of everyday life, but if I do not look back, I won't notice where God was especially present.

When I notice a particularly inspiring image or insight, I have a great place to start the next time I'm able to sit down and pray. See if you can develop a practice of evaluating a day and looking for signs of God's activity.

But we better look back while holding the hand of God. Our capacity for self-delusion is pretty amazing. Asking God to help us review will change the lenses, just like a new prescription can clear up physical vision. Asking God to shed light on our experiences means that we will see through new eyes. We may see completely overlooked insights when taking a few minutes to think about the highlights of our days.

> *Our capacity for self-delusion is pretty amazing.*

Over time, those few moments each day looking back will yield information about recurring patterns. The deeper meaning and successes of our accumulating days will be clearer.

This is not the same thing as making a list of our mistakes, shortcomings, or sins in preparation for the Sacrament of Reconciliation. Instead, this looking back is seeking to notice the graced moments—those instances where God was obviously at work and mysteriously present.

As you examine the recent days, consider these questions:

- *What activities brought me hope?*
- *What moments exuded joy?*
- *What energized me?*
- *When did I feel inspired?*

The answers to these questions will reveal God at work. Yes, God is busy, too; busy loving you and active in your life. The following questions will show you times when God was not the predominating influencer:

- *What depleted my energy?*
- *What was I trying to control?*
- *Where did I feel powerless or discouraged?*

Grace is something more easily recognized in retrospect. We ask God for the grace of time devoted to looking back. Praying for a grace is simply asking God for a gift. God loves to be asked for things.[8]

St. Ignatius believed wholeheartedly in this exercise of looking back. He called it an examen.[9] He told all who followed his spirituality to review daily where they had experienced the presence of God in their lives. After thanking God for all that is and inviting the Holy Spirit to grant insight and light, the persons at prayer ask Christ to walk back with them through the day.

---

[8] Matthew 7:7: "Ask, and you will receive. Seek, and you will find. *Knock,* and the door *will be opened* for you."

[9] Several excellent books are available on the examen, including Timothy M. Gallagher's *The Examen Prayer* (New York: Crossroads 2006).

Here are some questions to help you use this same process:

- *Where did I see Christ?*
- *What surfaces on its own, without stress or strain?*
- *Do I feel God heard me today?*
- *Did I hear anything that in retrospect I can identify as an insight from God?*
- *Did I get a sense that God knows where I am?*
- *Where did I miss an opportunity to see God?*

I pay attention to fleeting images, and see how I can resolve to make tomorrow an even closer walk with Jesus.

We may find ourselves responding: "Lord, I did not know, or anticipate, the gifts you had in mind for me yesterday."

Use your commute

Many of us are behind the wheel of a car every day commuting to and from work. This block of time can be put at the service of your desire to pray in a busy life. The trip to work can be focused on quiet, or on listening to music that praises God.

Some of us automatically turn on the news or a talk show while in the car. The radio may not be as helpful as well as some quiet time would be. Tom, a state employee, relates the morning of 9-11-2001 when, during his commute, he heard the radio newscaster say, "We will never get over this."

In his frustration at such a pessimistic attitude, he changed the station and heard a Hail Mary being recited over the airways.

He pulled the rosary out of his glove box, and that day he began a new habit.

"I have a short commute, so I can only complete half a rosary in the morning, and the other half on the way home, but I have never regretted this change in how I use my time," he explained, and he's been doing this now for more than ten years after the attack on the twin towers in New York.

"What I find by doing this is a new focus on Scriptural insights instead of the overturned truck on Highway 80."

Tom jokes about the "dead time" of listening to broadcast news, which is "horrid; it's all bad news. Do I really need to hear the details of a murder in a local neighborhood? I don't miss the news during my commute. I can get essential news in other ways. I find more calm by driving with a rosary in my hand."

Why not invest in a beautiful or significant-looking rosary that will attract you to picking it up and using it? Tom says he was getting "carpool tunnel" from using a ring-sized rosary that fit on a finger. He came across a rosary that is a single decade. This one is easy to use while driving and doesn't impede his hands or steering.

As his mind disengages from the distracting topics of news stories he could do without, he found he could welcome other ideas popping into his head. With the repetition of the mysteries of the rosary, scenes from Christ's life unfolded and he discovered deeper layers of meaning. He created space where God could even help him evaluate some aspect of his life.

> *Music operates at a deep level within us.*

Some people prefer the structure a recording provides, and in this case, you may wish to invest in one of the many recorded recitations of the rosary available. Listening to instrumental music can also offer a segue to prayer. Music can calm the busy spirit. Music operates at a deep level within us.

Inspirational seminars, Bible studies, books on tape, and other uplifting material provide additional options for turning your car into a cathedral.

The trip home offers time for looking back. It is time to ask yourself if you really need the radio or recorded media. If you forget to turn off the radio when the car stops, it automatically takes over the audio space when you return to the car and turn the key. A simple habit like turning off the radio before you turn off the car allows you to decide to add the radio to the ride home. It is not automatically, by default, on.

> *A few minutes of transition, in silence, can provide the fleeting moments needed to recover from the onslaught of the day's activity.*

A few minutes of transition, in silence, can provide the fleeting moments needed to recover from the onslaught of the day's activity. Sometimes God has been waiting all day for a silent moment to get a word in edgewise. Listen and don't be so quick to interrupt if God blesses you with silence. Wait for God and expect an insight.

Ask yourself, "Lord, where did you walk with me today?" Even five minutes devoted to this exercise can bring to your memory moments of great consolation that you may have missed otherwise. The "uh-oh" moments also come to mind, and you can ask God's forgiveness for those. Perhaps you can add a prayer for healing for the brokenness you may have caused. This is also a good time to resolve to try again to be a more loving person tomorrow. Perhaps you will discover you would like to make amends to someone, too.

Reviewing the day is not rehashing long past events that cannot be changed. That would be counterproductive and a waste of energy. Accept what happened, and recognize that the choices not chosen are "no longer an option." We should not be questioning decisions already made in ways that cause our progress to stagnate.

As I reflect back on my day, I sometimes discover that I spent time on something I could have skipped doing. Next time I'm tempted to jump thoughtlessly into a time waster, or to do someone else's job, I can remember this discovery, and take the time to say, "no, thank you."

When I invite God to shed light on the day just past, even the regretted choices are pointed out by such a loving hand that I often feel as if God gently puts an arm around my shoulder and says, "Dear one, my beloved, I love you despite what you did. Tomorrow you will do better, right?" When God points to an area where I made a mistake, the result is not self-condemnation, but an invitation to genuine sorrow. It's as if someone showed me a spill on the floor and handed me a bucket. I know what I need to do next.

As you make space for God to speak a word or two, God will generously respond. Allow God a crevice and God can create a canyon of love.

> *Looking back at the day takes courage, but God can be trusted to be gentle with you.*

Sometimes people fill their lives with busy activity to avoid having to see their mistakes, or to avoid changing from a destructive pattern. Looking back at the day takes courage, but God can be trusted to be gentle with you as you dare to review things that are difficult to face.

If you feel you *need* the radio, it may be a hint that you are running from something, or you have some subtle fear of what you might hear in the quiet. Be brave! Take a moment.

We are given here and now. Take advantage of this opportunity to be in the presence of God. Recognize that the Kingdom is here because God is here.

Give thanks, and resolve to be aware of where God IS in ordinary days and moments.

What a simple thing it is to take advantage of time alone in the car. The outside world is held at bay by the bubble of the car's interior. You can lock the doors and remain within. Here is a place to connect with God, praying for insight, offering thanks for small things that uplifted your heart today, and asking forgiveness for those places where you hurt someone. To close this time, again give thanks to God, and resolve to start fresh again tomorrow, learning from these moments of quiet.

Evaluate what you are thinking about

What do you want to think about every single day?

And how do you want to think about it?

It used to be when you asked someone, "How are you?" the common response was, "Fine, thanks. And you?" Now the most frequent response is, "Busy!" I am not sure when or how this happened, but it seems to miss the corresponding rhetorical question that asks how the questioner is. Concern for the other person's busy schedule flies out the window.

Perhaps the "Busy!" response admits to a certain selfishness on my part, as if to say, "I am consumed with thinking about my own cares right now. I can't be bothered with yours." Maybe not. But it's something to think about. Can we get back to feeling fine and reaching out with an inquiry about others? Or can we endeavor to be more than fine?

If you are feeling overwhelmed by a busy schedule, one helpful tip is to change how you think about what you do. Reframe your point of view.

One example is a 51-year-old sister who has multiple sclerosis. Knowing her, you would never say she *suffers* from M.S. Rather, after speaking with her, you would come away counting your own blessings of good health, and hoping to have an attitude like hers when you run up against the trials of your own life. Her life is full of joy and gratitude.

Every month this nun goes to what she calls her Spa Day. It is an MS treatment involving needles at a hospital that takes an hour and requires that she sit still, hooked to an IV. Now how many people would think, "Yay. I'm going to a hospital for a treatment!" This nun is one. She travels in her imagination out of the sterile hospital window to a place where she and God enjoy some beautiful scenery. She is grateful for a treatment that allows her to take a break from a very busy lifestyle as school principal, daily runner, and committed member of a large parish.

When you are feeling "I'm too busy!" in a bad way, think of a way to change your point of view. See if you can find an attitude of, "Lucky me!" God invites us to experience gratitude for everything, including what is unavoidable. A blessing from God is hiding there somewhere.

Find your own Spa Day in your active life.

Creating space

Really? ? It is not easy to reframe our thoughts. There are days when I do not feel like engaging in morning prayer, or in acting kindly, or in participating in the Liturgy. But I put my body into the church, or the prayer chair in my room, or I smile at the cashier and HOPE.

I hope that God will take my body, which I am placing in "the right" place, and pull my heart and mind and thoughts along. It is okay to be a failure, as long as I bring all of myself before the forgiving, accepting, healing God. God says, "I can work with that."

In chapter 5 I mentioned the idea of drawing an empty square in your journal as a way of quieting the constant stream of words that often makes up our prayer time. Nothing was to be written in there, remember? You are holding the space open so that God can come in. This, too, can offer a space of  hope. You can use this method of creating a pause in your day at other times, too. For example, during a long, dull meeting, you may find yourself doodling in the margin. Instead, draw a rectangle somewhere on that page.

The benefit of drawing a blank square is that it serves as a visual reminder that you have a relationship with Someone beyond this moment—your Creator. The blank shape on your page represents your willingness to go deeper into relationship with God and to let go of your thoughts and agenda while you listen for God's priorities. It is also something that merely appears like a doodle to someone seated next to you. Yet it is your secret code to yourself that you are aware that God is present in the moment. In that split second, what do you hear? Perhaps you will discover a feeling or a conviction that God loves you. Too often we forget this!

A few days pass, and you review your notes from the meeting as part of the workday. Suddenly you happen upon the blank rectangle that you used previously to dedicate a moment to say, "I love you, God," or where you simply became aware of the Almighty's presence. Now that shape on the page reminds you again: "God is my beloved. God is here, now." You can use this fresh moment to evaluate what is important, not only among your notes, but within your prayer experience since that meeting.

> *It only takes a few seconds to say hello to God...*

It only takes a few seconds to say hello to God, and you have done it!

A third party

Have you ever struggled with an issue and discovered that when you "talked it out" with someone, you achieved clarity that wasn't there before? Have you ever voiced something aloud and realized how silly it sounded? Then you have experienced already an inkling of the benefits that await you when you share your experiences at prayer with others. Sometimes another person can help you see where to make a small change, and be less busy.

Over the centuries, wise learners have discovered incredible benefits from sharing with another person what is happening during prayer. Spiritual direction is one method of deepening a sense of clarity regarding what is happening in one's relationship with God. [10]

The idea of talking about what happens during prayer with a fellow traveler on the spiritual adventure is increasing in popularity. Today people hunger for a genuine experience of God. And God loves to be talked about. Spiritual discussions have produced proven results for generations of Christians who seek to deepen their relationship with God and to discover what is truly important.

---

[10] Spiritual direction is a process that that helps a person discern the movement of God's Spirit in their life and how best to obey that Spirit. A director can offer support especially when important life decisions need to be made.

The benefits of confiding in another person are many. It may help us evaluate our next course of action. It may enlighten us to see a new path that we missed before. It may uncover an insidious plot aimed at our destruction.

St. Ignatius writes about evil's desire to operate in secret. When light is shed, evil behaves like a coward and takes flight. If evil can get us to keep our fears, doubts, and confusion to ourselves, it can dissuade us from good. Evil knows how to hide in the shadows, keeping us from repentance and forgiveness.

When we fear to reveal an experience or thought to another, it could be a sign that evil is trying to undermine us in the secret places of our soul. It is also possible for evil to use an overly busy schedule to prevent us from reflecting, from seeing that something in us needs to change.

If a course correction is needed, confiding in another person can open new inner avenues and point out the minefields we need to avoid if we want to grow closer to Christ.

Humans have the ability to trick ourselves into believing that our subtly twisted thinking is actually some insight from God. Sadly, we can deceive ourselves easily and ascribe pure motives to our not-so-pure actions. For example, a Eucharistic minister created a scandal at a parish I was in when he convinced himself that it was God's will for him to have an affair with a fellow Eucharistic minister even though both were married and had children.

Don't be too busy to check something out with a trusted and Godly friend.

Confiding our inmost thoughts to an experienced confessor or a spiritual director can shed light on our psyche, uncover hidden motivators, and help us discern what is coming from the true director, the Holy Spirit.

Choices

It takes a conscious choice to refuse to be mired in past shortcomings. It also takes a choice to step back for just a moment and think about how we are viewing ordinary situations.

It is not God who is asking us to do more or be more or give more. *God loves us in the moment and in who we are, knows every flaw, and cherishes us as we sleep, just as the parent who sneaks into the children's room and marvels at their beauty.*

> *God loves us in the moment and in who we are, knows every flaw, and cherishes us as we sleep, just as the parent who sneaks into the children's room and marvels at their beauty.*

But the temptation to lose perspective comes again as a new day announces itself with the alarm clock's buzz. The dates in your journal show that you lost a day somewhere. A cup of coffee may drag you into the day, and you "hit the road" again.

Choose to give yourself a break. That deep breath may be just the thing you need in this busy moment. Jesus asks us to lose ourselves in order to gain. Watch for those whispers during such crazy days, and take a five-second break. Look for the encouragement of Christ in a remembered Scripture passage or phrase.

A veggie drink's advertisement shows a person having made a choice to enjoy a less than satisfying snack. Suddenly they are hit with an insight, a "pow!" I find a similar wake up call grabbing me occasionally with a "pow! I could'a had a prayer moment!"

How do I react when I have such an insight, after the moment is past? Do I berate myself? Think less of me? Or do I accept the thwack of awareness with humility? I aim to do this more, and eliminate a wasted moment spent in front of a television commercial for a snippet of expressing love for my God. Reviewing past choices helps when new choices present themselves.

By the way...

Did you purchase that notebook as suggested in chapter 1? If so, take some time to review what you have written.

What? You haven't written anything? Well, don't beat yourself up about it. <u>Start fresh</u> today.

Grab a pen, and write, "Come Lord Jesus." And write the first thing that comes into your head, even if it's "I don't have any idea what to write." The next few sentences you write after that may begin a dialogue of discovery that will surprise you.

And you will be in the company of a great saint if you jot down your thoughts. St. Ignatius of Loyola used to derive great consolation, he wrote in his autobiography, from a little book he carried with him to write down his thoughts.

What words cause you to pause? One of the benefits of keeping a prayer notebook is the chance to reread it when you feel sad or discouraged. Busy people are very familiar with these emotions. Thoughts recorded in joyous times will uplift you when you are dry at prayer. When you're too busy, rereading your notes can remind you that you experienced happiness, and you will again.

Chapter 7

Distractions: Fleeting or festering?

It's early morning and it seems as if the sky is still rubbing the sleep out of its cloudy eyes. I gulp some coffee to wake me up and scan the morning prayer suggested in a devotional book.

Then I set the timer so I can meditate for 10 minutes. I sit in a comfortable position so I can forget about my body and endeavor to let go of all thoughts. I breathe deeply and gently shut my eyes.

The phone rings. My daughter needs a favor. We chat for a moment and I agree to help later in the week. After we hang up, I breathe deeply and gently shut my eyes again. Within a minute, my husband pops in to say goodbye; usually our brief meditation period coincides, so it's no interruption for him to come in and kiss me goodbye. Today he reminds me of a meeting at church he will be attending tonight.

As he leaves, I breathe deeply and gently shut my eyes again. The neighbor's dog barks as if something alarming is going on next door. My eyes fly open as I remember my promise to water their tomatoes while they are out of town this week. I jot a quick note, knowing that I may forget this task as the hubbub of the day moves into full throttle.

I breathe deeply and gently shut my eyes again. Within what feels like another minute a timer starts buzzing in the den. What in the world is that? I go to investigate and see that the computer had some internal alarm set to notify us of some critical update. As I resolve this issue I give up trying to meditate this morning, exasperated at "my failure" to "succeed" in quiet prayer.

Are these distractions or the stuff of prayer?

I remember a day when I sat down to meditate and the doorbell rang. I answered and felt dismay. On another occasion, a friend called in desperate need shortly after I sat down to pray silently. On a different day as meditation began I remembered a promise to be of service to someone. Due to circumstances like these, I was unable to spend time alone in silent prayer. Welcome to prayer as a busy person!

> *Welcome to prayer as a busy person!*

Were these distractions from prayer, or were they God's invitations to be a person of service? That friend needed a listener. My actions to be of service are also prayer.

Rather than be disappointed in myself for not taking time for prayer, I need to see that it is Christ who seeks my help when I am interrupted.

This is different from not even trying to spend time in quiet prayer. These distractions are responding to Christ in the surprising disguise of a person in need.

It's my expectations that get me into trouble. If I am too tied to what I plan to do, I see others as a distraction when in actuality they are themselves an experience of God loving me, or allowing me to love back. You see, not all distractions are bad. In fact, some are just where we need to be.

How do I learn to tell the difference between distractions that derail me and those that are gift? It takes time, and practice. Gentleness, too.

When it comes to setting aside a time for prayer, distractions are to be expected. How we react to them can trap us or help us find God in such moments.

If you are "a serious "prayer like me, this will sound familiar. You sit down to pray. Maybe you plan to spend five minutes doing nothing but repeating the name of Jesus and eliminating all thoughts from your mind in an effort to allow God in. Immediately you remember you are out of shave cream. The library book is overdue. That part to fix a broken hinge on the window arrived two days ago and you forgot to fix it. Your brother called yesterday because he lost his job. Your neighbor let his dog leave a calling card on your lawn again and you can smell it from your seat by the open window. Should you end the prayer session early to remove it?

How do you handle distractions at prayer? You have many options, and not all of them are good:

- *Get frustrated or angry with yourself for being unable to quiet your thoughts for five minutes.*
- *Give up after three minutes and start back to shorten that list of things to do.*
- *Judge yourself to be a failure at prayer and resolve **not** to bother setting aside five minutes tomorrow to engage in what feels like a waste of time.*
- *Intercede briefly for your brother, and gently move your mind back to the simple repetition of Jesus' name. Perhaps God allowed you to think of your brother just now so that you would remember to pray for him.*
- *Ask God to give you the time you need later to fix the window or pick up after the neighbor's dog. And once again, try to put it out of your mind, just as sticks float down a river while from the shore you focus on the stream just in front of you.*

- *Put a pen and paper near your prayer chair to jot down "important" distracting thoughts.*
- *Resolve to add two minutes to this immediate prayer time, especially if you don't feel like doing it. If it is an evil spirit that is filling your head with distractions in an attempt to discourage you, this technique is very effective to drive away distracting thoughts.*
- *Laugh at yourself. Scripture says we are earthen vessels, and we all know how cracked and imperfect pottery can be. Laugh at your inability to stay focused for even five minutes, and*
- *Thank God for loving you just as you are. God is present, even if you can't feel any proofs of this fact.*

Distractions can steal time from us outside of prayer as well, making us feel more frenetic outside of our formal moments of prayer. Then, as the day unfolds, we allow the distractions from our greater priorities to destroy our peace of mind. Is that really what God wants for me? I don't think so.

How many times have I digressed into a long daydream in a distraction! I catch myself several minutes later, wondering where my mind went. I *should* be doing the important thing, but instead I find myself distracted into the unimportant one. I clench my teeth and stew over what is left undone. Someone told me this is "*shoulding*" on yourself.

Some interruptions could be God's gentle reminders that we are to love our neighbors and be of service before all else. These are the times when I am called to be the Good Samaritan on the road. In that parable,

> *I am called to be the Good Samaritan on the road.*

Jesus applauds the Samaritan who gave up his own agenda, whatever that was, and stopped to help a stranger.[11]

Perhaps the genuine call to prayer lives in the interruptions. God knows what we are going through. And God is all about relationships. When we enter into relationship with Christ, he brings along everybody—needy, grubby, hurtful, and inconvenient people. He even invites me to consider people who normally might seem repugnant to me.

All of this doesn't mean we should stop trying to spend time in silent prayer. On the contrary, we need to keep making the efforts to be with God when life gets particularly busy.

And we must not beat up ourselves when our efforts appear to be pointless. Some people are very good at this, especially when normal distractions surface. Are busy people more familiar with this trap? When we catch ourselves in choosing a lesser good, we can regret the choice and move on. God does not condemn us nor lead us to despair. The loving, gentle God is not as tough on people as people are on themselves.

We need to discern carefully if we are creating obstacles to silent prayer ourselves, or whether distractions are invitations to listen to the active God who invites us to co-create the world.

If you believe that God is inviting you to some action when you are distracted, then trust that God is doing some miracle within them. God honors our intentions, so even if we "misdiagnose" a distraction and chase off in the "wrong" direction, God knows how to make all things right again.

---

[11] Luke 10:29-37.

As the New Living Translation of Romans 8:28 says, "We know that God causes everything to work together for the good."

This is true even when we are distracted, make mistakes, or even when we fail.

On the other hand

Not all interruptions and distractions are from a good source. When evil spirits cannot keep us from doing good, then their efforts turn toward distracting us, wearing us out, or getting us to do some *lesser good* than *the great good* that God intends.

Have you heard that if you place a frog in boiling water that it will jump right out? But if you put a frog in tap water, and slowly turn up the heat, he will boil to death before he realizes the temperature was slowly rising. The same is true when evil uses a small wedge against us. A small distraction that we follow, or fondle, or allow to take root deep within can grow into something we will later have to work hard to weed out.

I know it's not easy to make time to pray. I know it can be discouraging. I also know that I must never give up trying. And I must forgive myself when I fail, and forgive others who disappoint me. More on that later.

Think before you act

Action is meant to flow from prayer. It doesn't seem to be that way for me. Usually, I act, then ask God to bless what is done. Before beginning that new task, I ought to pause. Think. If my life were to end today, is this the very next task I would want to undertake now? Maybe that sounds very dramatic, but St. Ignatius offers this as one possible way of making choices.[12]

I find I am easily distracted into lesser priorities while evading the things that I claim are most important to me. Sometimes this happens when I am especially tired, or when I am tempted by some "shiny object."

Why am I so distractible from my greater priorities?

Many of us live today as if we had an unlimited future here. At my quilters group, someone brought in all the unfinished projects of a woman who had passed away. Lots of beautiful scraps lay on the table, and I began to pick up greedily a pile of beautiful fabrics. An 80-year-old woman in our group, a woman of charming wisdom, shook her head and said, "I would have to live another 200 years to finish the projects *I already have* in my sewing room at home! I certainly can't take on any more of these projects."

She caused me to pause. I, too, have a sewing cupboard full of ideas, patterns, fabrics, and inspirations. With all I already have, I would need to live perhaps another 100 years to complete most of them. These new fabrics were a distraction. I edited the pile of scraps in my hand to a select few, but the words of my wise quilter friend repeated themselves in my mind all week long.

What if each of us lived as if we only had another 200 days on the earth? What changes would you make to what you will do today? Would you let yourself get distracted into this or that project? What if you were only to live another 20 days? What would you have wanted to do today? What if 20 hours

---

[12] The Spiritual Exercises of St. Ignatius offer suggestions for making decisions, including imagining that you are on your deathbed years from now. What decision will you wish to have made as you look back on today?

from now you get hit by a bus? What would you have wanted to do in the next 20 hours?

I think about my daughter going through my sewing stash, tossing scraps with a shake of her head. "What in the world was Mother thinking when she saved *this*?" If I were present, I would tell her that those labels are going to make a fabulous postage stamp quilt some day. But will some day ever arrive?

> *What if you were only to live another 20 days? What would you have wanted to do today?*

I suspect that busy people like me overestimate what they can accomplish, making lists where half the items carry over, undone, onto tomorrow's list.

What do you have stuffed into a drawer, collecting dust in a corner, or waiting in a closet for your attention? Think about my wise quilter friend, and do something important today!

What do you feel is important? A kind word to a stranger that pays itself forward in other kindnesses will transform the world over time. This, too, is prayer. A smile instead of a self-centered, stressed-out comment can brighten someone's entire day.

We can grow if we can take a few minutes to think, and then ask God for the graces, and self-discipline, to choose the more important thing to do right now. Then start doing it, maybe by telling yourself that you will just devote 15 minutes to it. Give yourself permission to walk away from the task after that 15 minutes. It just might happen that you willingly choose to continue working on it when that first 15 minutes passes.

Suddenly you are enjoying tackling this important priority of your day. Maybe not. Either way, you can feel a greater sense of peace, knowing that you chose while metaphorically holding on to the hand of God. It is a peace "the world cannot give."[13] Only God can provide genuine peace. Sometimes, we have to think, ask, act and then embrace the free gift of peace that follows.

Standing in line

Modern life is full of distractions. My smartphone is a big one for me. I can play games lasting for a few seconds (pause and play later) or for a few hours. And we do need to relax!

I wonder how I can be better at choosing to relax through prayer. I do feel so much better after reading Scripture, but it's tough to set the other distracting activities aside.

When waiting in line for a cashier, out comes my phone. I can check email, text, and search the internet all while I wait in line. My mind becomes absorbed in something to distract me from the long wait. Meanwhile music drones over the store sound system. I would never choose those tunes. I can tune it out. I can focus into the phone. I don't get as frustrated at the length of time I have to wait. And if I glance at the others in line, I see that they, too, are all on their phones. Have you experienced that?

> *Busy people grab moments wherever we can.*

Busy people grab moments wherever we can. And our spirits can be neglected. I like to turn waiting moments into prayerful moments.

For example, instead of reaching for a game, I use one of the many apps available on the phone to read about the saint of

---

[13] Notice the Gospel of John 14:27: "Peace I leave with you; my peace I give you. I do not give to you as the world gives. Do not let your hearts be troubled and do not be afraid."

the day or to pray the liturgy of the hours. Even the whole Bible is available at usccb.org. No one needs know what I am up to as I wait in line. I can put in my earbuds and listen to Christian music. Or, if I can find the discipline to leave my phone in my pocket, I can pray silently for the cashier or perhaps offer a prayer for the strangers ahead of me in line. Every one of them carries a burden of one sort or another.

I close my eyes and use a brief moment to check in with myself. I can review how I treated people during the last hour. I peek occasionally so I move when the line inches forward. I examine what I'm feeling right now, physically, emotionally, or mentally. Sometimes I just imagine the face of God looking at me right now as my eyes remain closed.

This takes some serious concentration to let go of the surrounding distractions. I encourage you to try it. A few moments in line could open a door to a potentially new perspective for you. God just may choose to grab this fleeting moment to provide you with some surprising insight. All of this is possible while waiting.

Distractions seem to be the norm for a busy life, and that includes prayer. Learn to expect distractions, to acknowledge them, and to quit trying so desperately to eradicate them.

I feel so much calmer when I accept the interrupting phone call and the request from someone for help in a moment I did not anticipate. Yes, interruptions or distractions may be God's invitation to put your prayer into action.

Don't go looking for distractions. If they appear, evaluate them and treat them as the individual circumstances suggest. Deal with them and move on.

When I endeavor to quiet my mind and listen to God, my mind fills up with the things I should do, could do, would have done, or wish I was doing. Such distractions are inevitable, but it doesn't mean we should chase them, harbor them, or allow them to fester inside of us in ways that leave us feeling frustrated.

> *There is a difference between a distraction that leads us toward God, and one that leads us away. Check out the results of the distraction for clues to its source.*

There is a difference between a distraction that leads us toward God, and one that leads us away. Check out the results of the distraction for clues to its source. You will learn through several experiences which ones help you and which ones hinder you. If the fruits of the experience are good, then the distraction probably was an invitation from God. If you feel discouraged, and robbed, then that situation—or how you handled it—was not from God, who loves beyond measure and gives hope, not harm.[14]

Sometimes the things that appear as distractions are the very stuff I need to pay attention to in prayer. So before I rush past the distractions, I am learning to turn them over to the Lord, whether as intercessory prayers, or as a conversation starter. And sometimes, the Lord just helps me let them go.

Pray first, act second

The best thing to do, according to St. Catherine of Siena, is to pray first, and then act. Pretty often, I take action and then realize I am rushed, overburdened, or off track. Sometimes I

---

[14] Jeremiah 29:11 reads, "I know the plans I have for you, says the Lord. Plans to prosper you and not to harm you, plans to give you hope and a future."

agree to do something and halfway through working on it, I remember to ask God to help me. I've done it backwards again! It's another instance of, "Listen, Lord, your servant is speaking," rather than the opposite attitude, expressed in 1Samuel 3:10.

Put another way, "Prayer begets action, not the other way around," according to Dean Brackley, S.J. "Action is most human when it is a grateful response." [15]

Ideally, our activity should come out of our prayer. If you are not in a habit of praying before acting it is okay! God can work with that. God can work with anything (all things work together for good, writes St. Paul in Romans 8:28). It's also okay to pause and ask, "God, how did I get to feeling so busy today?"

Then wait with no agenda other than to clear your mind and listen. What does God want to tell you in this pause? What would God want you to hear about the choices that keep you busy? God wants to be consulted, included, acknowledged, invited, and ultimately loved. Even if all you are offering God is a brief moment between other rushed moments.

I'm often surprised by an idea that pops independently into my head. Sometimes I shrug and the puzzled look on my face remains. Perhaps that is God inspiring me via some distracting thought.

Do you believe that God can deepen your relationship with each other as you begin to invest snippets of time into thoughtfulness of God?

God can take seemingly insignificant efforts and build something greater. And great.

---

[15] See *The Call to Discernment in Troubled Times*, p.246, n. 4.

Chapter 8

Story moments

Everyone has one; learn from stories

Stories come in many forms. Everyone loves a good story. *Some stories are prayers.* Entering into other people's stories helps us see the hand of God at work and calls us away from self-absorption. In fact, sometimes it is easier to see grace in action outside of our own situations. That's why it is easier to give advice than to take it ourselves. I learn from the experiences of others, and I discover new insights through these images of God. Because that is what each of us are.

Just listening to someone's story, or to their immediate moment's preoccupation, is prayer. Take a new step: as you listen, ask God to help you listen. What is unsaid—the feelings, body language, my own preconceived ideas? Pay attention and bring that into the conversation, if appropriate. Together we discover strength and encouragement.

Stories in the daily news can be depressing when we hear about tragedies all over the globe. Rev. Bernie Brannon, S.J., used to pray briefly for the people behind the headlines as he read the paper. We can do this, too. It might be victims of war, pensioners whose income is cut, and homicide victims and the perpetrators. Bernie used to offer brief, instantaneous prayers as he read. He reframed his approach to the newspaper by bringing an awareness of God into it. Hearing or reading the news generated fleeting moments of prayer. Bernie now reads the headlines from heaven.

In addition to newspapers, could you think about praying while reading email, listening to a professor, watching TV news, or in other daily encounters?

"How are you?" is a common question we ask one another. The usual responses rarely seem to call forth a genuine dialogue. Yet even in a simple response ("I didn't sleep well," "I could be better," and the popular response today, "Busy!") we are receiving an opportunity to pray for that person. What if I take another's response to "how are you?" as an invitation to gently turn to Christ who walks with us? I can ask God to bless them. This prayer need not be spoken out loud. It can be your little secret with God. No one needs to know that you are praying the other person's story.

> *...Could you think about praying while reading email messages?*

When people give you glimpses into their lives, imagine that during the conversation, Christ is standing between you. Instead of just smiling and nodding, try to imagine Christ as part of this conversation, and gently, silently, ask God to help this person with whatever occupies them. Nothing need be said aloud in this exercise. Simply turn to your brother, Jesus, inside your thoughts, and say something like, "What about this Jesus? Will you step in and help?"

For some people, this will be a difficult habit to cultivate. It will take discipline and practice. For others, it will cause you to stretch your imagination. The ability to create ideas and concepts in our head is, I believe, one of the ways in which we are an image of the Creator.

Taking time to listen to your own story

I use my imagination in prayer. I give myself permission to pray my own story. Try this:

Close your eyes and sit where you will not be interrupted for at least five minutes. It is time to tell yourself a story. Make it personal.

Wait a minute, you say. *I can't take five minutes.* Remember to schedule an appointment on your calendar for yourself. You deserve a five-minute break. Trust me; your whole day will go better.

Begin by imagining a place, perhaps based on an actual location, where you expect to encounter peace. Perhaps it is a hillside or a shore or a fireside cabin. It doesn't have to be a real place, but if conjuring up a favorite locale helps you, by all means try it. Scripture suggests several possibilities, including images of water and boats. Settle in and "see" this place where a part of your story is about to take place.

Imagine that you are alone in this beautiful place, and just rest in its beauty.

Then imagine that Jesus walks up to you, or appears suddenly next to you, and sits down comfortably at your side.

What does Christ say to you? Imagine how he looks at you. What would you say to him?

Take some time to just sit quietly together. Do not rush the moment. Good friends can sit silently and enjoy the view.

Then thank Jesus for coming to visit.

When you are ready to return to the present moment, give God thanks. Promise yourself that you can return to this place another day. Open your eyes and breathe deeply and slowly.

If you have time, write a few thoughts about what just happened, even if it is just questions.

Jesus was a storyteller. As you think about your personal story, consider his. What can you learn from Jesus' own stories and human experiences? Can you imitate Jesus as he listens? As he reacts to people? We read about our larger, family throughout Scripture.

Try using Christ's life as a starting point for your quiet five-minute storytelling session. You could start by reading one of the Gospels until a story strikes you. Then imagine yourself *in* the story. Be one of the characters. Allow Christ to speak to your circumstances right now. Try to carry that story with you all day.

> *What can you learn from Jesus' own stories and human experiences?*

The Bible is a great place to be inspired to pray. At a Bible study a spiritual director suggested looking up the Scriptures corresponding to your birth date. Not every book in the Bible will have as many chapters as months in the year, but if you were born on 5/1, for example, you may find Matthew 5:1 consoling for you: "Blessed are the poor in spirit." Try it just for fun. What you read may surprise you.

83

It is true that many times we turn to Scripture hoping for inspiration and discover... nothing. Words don't leap from the page and inspire us to set the world on fire. This happens when friends converse, too. Sometimes we run out of things to say and we just sit in each other's company.

When you are void of insights during prayer, feel free to shrug your shoulders and say, "well, Lord, I tried to be present to you in prayer. Here I am. Nothing's happening on this end that I can see. In faith, I trust you are here, even though I hear zip." Press on with your day.

God knows how and where to find you.

Was Jesus this busy?

Jesus was quite busy, in my opinion. Reference the stories in Matthew 14:19-36 (or in Mark 6:41-56). First, he feeds a huge crowd. Then he heals pretty much everyone in sight. Oh, and he teaches the crowd at length.

I can imagine him dismissing the crowd, and people coming up to see him personally, like when people mob a priest after Mass. It takes a while for the crowd to disperse. Only then does Jesus get to expend a great deal of energy praying all night.

> *God understands my busy choices, and loves me unconditionally through them. I can, tongue in cheek, ask God to help me walk on water when I need to catch up.*

He sent the disciples on ahead of him in the boat, remember? Scripture says that it was the fourth watch of the night when he tried to catch up with his pals by walking on water. The fourth watch is between 3 and 6 a.m. He didn't have time for the conventional crossing; he was cramming in an all-nighter of prayer. So he cheated the clock by catching up with his disciples by walking on water! Nearly scared *them* to death.

I take consolation from my perhaps fractured interpretation of Christ's ministry. The bottom line is: God understands my busy choices, and loves me unconditionally through them. I can, tongue in cheek, ask God to help *me* walk on water when I need to catch up with people and be where I'm supposed to be but am running behind.

Take time to think about Peter, who bravely leaves the security of the comfortable boat to surge onward with Christ, only to be thwarted by fear. How often am I shortchanging myself with fear? Do I cry out to the Lord, "Save me!" when my busy lifestyle overwhelms me?

When I have too much to do, I can freely and with expectant faith yell out, "Lord, save me!" and know that Christ can calm the storm of emotions within and join me in the boat that feels like it's sinking. Christ is in my story.

Another story: walking on water

Are you too busy to let go? The Scriptural image of Jesus as the Living Water suggests a story to help you converse with God about your busy life. [16] Adapt the following to your own circumstances. Find a comfortable spot and consider:

> *God is a river refreshing the soul. Imagine the love of God as a body of water wider than the Mississippi. God's flowing, encompassing love floods our hearts. This is a God who allows us the freedom to wade, but when we surrender, sweeps us off our feet.*

---

[16] John 4:14. At the well in Samaria, Jesus promises to quench our thirst in a spring that wells up to eternal life.

Imagine that the current of God who is love is carrying us places we never expected. Think about those areas in our lives where we can let go and let God—when we are in the deepest part of the river, able to sink into God with total trust and breathe as if we were a fish. Trust in God over this area of our lives is complete. Perhaps this depth doesn't fit anything in your life right now. It's okay.

Maybe you find yourself in a beautiful, narrow, tree-shaded spot where you seem to be caught in an eddy. You float around in circles, going nowhere. If you are like me, you want to see progress, so this can be a frustrating place to be. Relax. God knows you are here.

Or you observe the flow of the great river sweeping past while you are in a sheltered bay off to the side. Imagine your problems floating by. You may need to ask God for the courage to let them pass.

In what areas of your life are you standing knee-deep in love, but still firmly grounded and in control, unwilling to let go of your own ego? God lets us stand there.

At other times, you have the courage to wade in further, trusting God enough to be in up to our waist, but still with feet firmly planted.

Have you ever felt you were in up to your neck in God's will for you, and in God's love?

Are you too busy to go with the flow of love?

Imagine you are swept off and out of control. God leads. You are like a tiny leaf on a torrent. Why do we live as if we could direct this river! God's covenant is unbreakable, yet how we become broken when we throw ourselves against it.

As a speck on the water, you may find yourself to be further downstream than is comfortable.

Are you behaving like salmon? During spawning season, salmon struggle against the river, expend all of their energy trying to go opposite the flow, and die in the end. Check in with yourself and see if you can detect ways where you fail to surrender to God's lead. Endeavor to allow yourself to be carried away in grace.

Now some readers will say, "I can't set aside time for this." Okay. Try a one-minute meditation instead. Take a few moments to think about your own blood flowing through your body. Find your pulse. Listen to its rhythm. Force yourself to hold your wrist and your pulse for a full minute, eyes shut, and picture the work your blood goes through while we typically take it for granted. Breathe deeply to give oxygen to your blood. Then thank God for the cells which are rushing through your wrist. And off you go!

A quick break can bring a moment to recover from a hectic schedule. When I can make such a break a daily habit, I begin to notice a leaning toward a more peaceful composure. I also notice a subtle change in my attitude.

Over time, you may be able to grow this prayer break into two minutes, and then three.

> *A quick break can bring a moment to recover from a hectic schedule.*

Let's move to yet another example of using your imagination during prayer. Remember you are developing a habit, and don't judge your efforts. You are developing a healthy practice, like exercising flabby muscle.

Allow the river to undergo a transformation in your mind. It becomes a bloodstream (yes, a stream) that courses to every area of a human body, flooding each part with life. Picture yourself floating in the bloodstream. The various parts of any human body are kept alive by the refreshing action of the blood. The heart pumps the replenishing blood to every part of the body.

You are part of a bigger body—the church— where all people are connected. The old saying, "They say it runs in his blood," comes to mind here. Imagine yourself making a trip to the cleansing Sacred Heart. Whether you travel to the fingertips and toes of your world, be still and confident that you are on your way back to the Heart to be cleansed, refreshed, and propelled outward on a mission. Christ is source of this circulation system, providing the energy to move back and forth. Where does God send you out and when will you be circulated back?

When the blood visits the various extremities of the body, it becomes soiled and depleted and it must return through the action of the pumping Heart to the center where it will be cleansed before it is sent out again.

Christ's own blood invigorates us in the Eucharist. You do run in his blood. The next time you are moving forward to receive communion, perhaps this image of traveling within an artery in the body of Christ will come to your mind, connecting your Sunday worship to an ordinary day in your week. When you hold your pulse for 60 seconds on a busy weekday, remember who you are. Christ is in your blood and you are in his. The meal that is shared is a joining in the body of God. Look around you. When you enter into Christ, he brings everybody along with him. None are beyond the reach of God.

A story about keys—ways to unlock busy days

Let me tell you one of my personal stories. I'm one of those people whose stress from busy schedules tends to result in a stiff neck, grinding teeth at night, and sore shoulders. And I try a little harder, expend greater effort, and try to get a grip.

But then something happens to add some new task to my plate, or I spend time searching for a misplaced phone or other lost object. It becomes apparent how little control I really have. How does a busy person like me learn *to let go*?

One morning, I got to the car without my keys, and after searching my purse, I realized I must have left them in the chapel, where I had just stopped for a quick visit before the Blessed Sacrament. Did you ever lose your keys and experience that terrible, sinking feeling which includes such loss of control?

I returned to the chapel and thankfully, the keys were on the pew. I picked them up and I knelt in overwhelming gratitude, keys lifted on palms up and open.

And it came into my head: "Have you put these keys, and what they open, into My Hands?"

I looked down into my hands. I held the key to my house, my car, and my office. It was an insightful moment for me. These were the "keys" to what I valued in life.

> *God invites us to trust more fully.*

"Okay. I give these keys and what they represent to you, Lord. Help me give control to you."

God invites us to trust more fully. Since that day, I have placed my keys at various times in my outstretched palm and reminded myself that only God truly holds the keys to my life. It only takes a moment to lift the keys heavenward.

We talk about a key ingredient, or the key to success. Keys represent control and sometimes power; the one with the keys is trusted. At my church, only a chosen few have the key to the community center. At work, I have to sign for them. People who have keys usually are persons in authority, at least in regard to the place or item that they can open. And in Scripture, we find this key analogy as well.

Keys in and of themselves can be pretty tiny. Yet they grant access to mansions, yachts, factories, and metaphorically human hearts, which are infinite spaces holding the Infinite God.

Key of David is a title of Christ that often surfaces during Advent. [17] If you meditate on the meaning of keys using your own physical key ring, a goal could be to create a trigger from the physical world to a concept in the spiritual world. Before you turn a key in a lock, you may find yourself considering the key to your own heart.

After losing my keys *again* (do other busy people lose things as often as I do when I rush about?) and finding myself locked out of pretty much everything, I began to get a new understanding of what it means for Jesus to be my key. Eternity is not so far away. We have an easily accessible key to get us there.

Beyond the stories

As you practice prayers of imagination and use the little things in your day, even keys, you will uncover images that bring peace or consolation. It is wise to return to such images again and again.

The stories in our imaginations can lead us to a real letting go. The previous examples in this chapter are what some people call contemplative prayer: focusing on a story or an

---

[17] Isaiah 22:22 talks about the authority of the one who holds the key to the house of David. The words in verse 22 are echoed again in Revelation 3:7. The O Antiphons each refer to a title for Christ and are used especially during the last seven days of Advent. They also appear in the hymn "Oh Come, Oh Come, Emmanuel."

image and sinking deeper into imagination and by this means drawing closer to God.

Another method of prayer moves beyond and outside stories and imagination. Meditation is an effort to let go of everything so that God has room to do *all* the "talking." Busy people may find this kind of prayer difficult because we are distracted by activities needing to be done. Yet meditation, even in small doses, can restore your spirit. See if this works for you:

Set aside some time for prayer. Close your eyes. Imagine you are floating effortlessly, perhaps in a pool. If you are not a good swimmer, imagine you are on a supporting raft. The water temperature is perfect. It offers no distraction to your letting go. Attempt to empty your mind of all thoughts, distractions, to-do lists, and concerns. Do you remember ever floating on your back in a pool with your eyes closed against the burning sun? All sounds were muted as your ears rested gently, just below the water's surface, and noises became distant, though present.

During this prayer, tensions, expectations for yourself and others, and the external environment fade. You are at rest. When you think about something—anything— picture it as an object sinking away from you. Listen to the quiet.

Let go of the image of the pool as best you can, so that your mind is empty. As thoughts "float" into your mind, acknowledge them but then permit them to depart. Sometimes ideas linger, and you have the opportunity to look gently at them before you allow them to pass out of view. Let yourself be alone with God. Repeating the name of Jesus in your mind may help dismiss all thoughts.

An image or insight may gently present itself during this time, but watch out that you are not giving in to some distraction disguised as an insight. If you find yourself planning, problem solving, or listmaking, you are being sidetracked from this type of meditation.

Some people focus on their breathing and slow it down. Others repeat a single word over and over again until it seems to lose all meaning. Use whatever helps you to relax and allows your constantly busy brain to empty even further.

> *At the conclusion, you may feel no different. It may appear that nothing happened at all.*

Some people set a timer for 10 minutes so that they're not distracted by wondering, "How long have I been sitting here?" Before you end this prayer time and open your eyes, simply thank God. At the conclusion you may feel no different. It may appear that nothing happened at all during this time. But God may surprise you later in the day or week. Be patient. God may use this self-emptying time to wash away hurts, hydrate your soul, or quench your impatience for results.

Let go of stress

Prayerful storytelling and meditation not only aid relaxation, but they also reduce stress. They make use of qualities in an acronym for something busy people seek: BLISS. It stands for Breathe. Let go. Imagine beauty (use imagery). Stretch. Smile.[18]

Modern medicine confirms that stress kills. Reducing it makes for happier lives while at the same time creating room for prayer. But it is not easy to be still. Keep trying.

---

[18] The Biofeedback Service of the Department of Psychiatry, University of New Mexico School of Medicine, suggests breathing, letting go, shaking, and imagery to aid relaxation. I added "smile!" to create the mnemonic, bliss. Many other relaxation techniques are available in the health care profession.

It may appear to you that time spent in such emptying exercises is a waste. Results aren't always apparent. It may take months to notice a change. It's difficult to measure an experience like this on the cultural yardstick of accomplishments. Don't give up! It takes trust in God to believe that, even if it seems as if this was completely useless, you will soon experience new possibilities of grace. When you least expect it, grace will flourish thanks to your prayerful story.

Have faith that God is working within you. Keep your eye out for an instance much later in your day when you discover you were patient when normally you would have exploded, or when some other virtue was apparent and you found yourself asking, "Where did that virtue come from?"

Share your story

Some of us have the support of a good, prayerful spouse. Many couples are inspired by one another to pray. A man's daily meditation period is a witness to his wife.

Others are alone, but they have the encouragement of a regular small group that holds them accountable to continuing their efforts to pray. Some are able to meet individually with a spiritual director, who accompanies them in their prayer journey.

God wants us to be in community with one another.

Still others don't have the support of a community. If you don't have someone or some group with whom you can share your faith story, find one. God wants us to be in community with one another. Such a support is like lifeblood and we draw strength from one another. Don't be afraid to call upon others when you are feeling rushed. The body really is there to serve you. Nobody need go it alone. Priests, confessors, spiritual directors, parish nurses, grief support ministries, faith sharing groups, and more are available to strengthen us when times get a little rough.

People feel a shyness that prevents them from speaking about spiritual things despite living in a culture that pries regularly into our private business. Formerly taboo topics are headline news and broadcasters show no qualms about reporting on celebrities' sex lives. How ironic that we seem to clam up when it comes to conversations about God. We are afraid of what people will think. And evil wants to squelch any conversations about God. It takes some courage to speak about spiritual things, but the benefits are longlasting for a busy person. It is surprising how many people welcome a subtle invitation to speak about God, prayer, a Higher Power, or some related aspect of these topics. We all need support, and it is wise to seek it out.

My husband and I participate in a bimonthly faith-sharing group. This group inspires us. The group also holds us accountable. We know that when we meet, the first question will be about how we noticed God at work in our lives since we last met. I hear awe-inspiring anecdotes about how Christ was present, worked small miracles, and challenged individuals in the group to some deeper truth. If I have ignored God for the past two weeks, the group is gentle with my shortcomings, and they will pray for me. Amazing graces abound.

Sharing your story with others is not only a blessing for them; it's a graced encouragement for the one who is telling the tale. And God is listening, too.

Chapter 9

"Wow!" moments: Who inspires you?

God wants the prayer time we seek even more than we want it for ourselves. Our primary inspiration for prayer is perhaps obvious: it is God, the Great Initiator. So when you set out to pray, *ask for God's help and inspiration*. Ask, expecting that this request will be answered, and then be on the lookout for the answer. It may come when you least expect it, and perhaps during the busiest part of your day.

Steven Covey recommends to "begin with the end in mind."[19] And in this case, begin your prayer with the goal of a closer relationship with God in your mind. Do you think God can be outdone in generosity? Of course not! Ask God for a closer relationship. Allow God to "wow" you.

Be on the lookout for God to inspire you.

We don't always notice miracles because we take for granted a good night's rest, the sun, good health, and so much more. These are miracles, occurring in every moment.

"Ask and you will receive," we read in Luke 11:9-10. Ask to be inspired by God to make whatever changes are in your

---

[19] In *The 7 Habits of Highly Effective People* (rev. ed. [New York: Free Press, 2004]), author Steven Covey explains that things are created twice: once when we envision them, and then again when they actually happen.

best interest and which will bring about release from feeling too busy. Ask to see miracles, to be inspired. My dad used to say, "Be careful what you wish for, because you will surely attain it." Beginning with the end in mind is important.

Take a few minutes to ponder people who inspire you. Are they themselves miracles? Who are your role models, and are you doing anything to emulate their qualities? Are you finding that you actually do the opposite of what these mentors would do? Nobody is perfect, but sometimes we behave carelessly and follow the wrong ideals. In other words, we enact values which really don't represent what we admire.

Who are your favorite saints?

> *Take a few minutes to ponder people who inspire you.*

Their example may have touched your heart over the years. They are friends, even though they are in heaven already. Famous or not, they inspire us to new determination to imitate them.

Invite them to pray for and with you, and talk to them. Why not? Everyone can use a little help, especially busy people. Why not enlist the support of the cream of the crop?

In your prayer notebook, write down the names of some of your favorite saints, followed by the words, "pray for us." Spend a moment in friendship with like-minded holy ones and allow yourself to be encouraged by their points of view. Be sure to include St. Paul, a busy tentmaker, preacher, and prolific writer who made three extensive missionary journeys and one long circuitous trip to Rome. And be sure to include Martha on your list. I think Lazarus' sister is the patron saint for busy people. [20]

---

[20] See Luke 10:38-42

Inspiring reading

Taking up a book is another way of finding inspiration and encouragement to make time for prayer. You may find that a few lines in a book cause you to come up with your own inspiring tangents. Yes, reading can be a form of prayer.

For example, I was reading "The Way of Perfection," by St. Theresa of Avila. She talks about our souls as having many rooms, or mansions. I realized that I have opened some rooms in my soul to God, but I have locked rooms in my soul, too.

I put the book down and pondered. Like so many busy people, I would rather control things myself than abandon myself to the unknown result when God is in charge. Some of my inner rooms hold scary secrets that I am unwilling to face, including some truths about my own sinful habits I would rather not investigate. If I do, I may have to change!

This great Carmelite saint inspired me to a new contemplative prayer. It goes like this: I imagine I have a large key ring, the kind jailors keep, and on it are all the keys to the rooms I keep locked. The ring is heavy. It is a burden and a barrier to my freedom. Keeping parts of myself "locked" away from God is a real lack of trust on my part.

I explore the areas where I find it difficult to trust God. Some days, it's work. "See you later, God, I've got this covered." And usually it's my morning commute and driving in general. As I imagine the jail's ring, I remember that person I cannot forgive.

I allow my posture to change. I lift my palms open before God and imagine that God is lifting that weighty ring of keys out of my tired hands. God takes control of the agenda and decides which room to unlock. I can trust that God will not unlock the rooms I am not yet ready to enter. God knows my limitations better than I do. God knows my strength, and like most people, usually I underestimate it. God knows what I can take, and sometimes wants to show me a hidden strength deep inside.

I may give the keys to God, but I've got to watch out for signs that I've taken them back later in the day (old habits die hard). I hear the keys jangling in my pocket again. Can I laugh at myself when I find that I'm carrying that burden again? I don't have to carry it. God can be trusted to help me unlock the rooms, and to take me by the hand to lead me out when I resist leaving a prison cell behind. God loves me as I approach the shortcomings and secrets hidden within. But it is difficult to rededicate all of me to Christ.

I must ask God for the grace to *want* to be free. I need God to work with me on this one. I invite God to inspire a new openness within despite my resistance to change.

A busy leader

St. John Paul II, who died at 85, is an inspiring role model for busy people. During his 26 years as pope, he traveled to 100 countries, made 146 pastoral visits within Italy, and visited 317 of Rome's 333 parishes. He had 38 official visits with government personalities, 738 meetings with heads of state, and 246 audiences with prime ministers. He participated in 19 World Youth Days. Was he the busiest pope ever?

His most important documents include 14 encyclicals, 15 apostolic exhortations, 11 apostolic constitutions, 45 apostolic letters, and 5 published books. Rather than take the rest a man over 80 might consider well earned, he spent himself in service

...Sometimes a full agenda is unavoidable, inescapable. In fact, sometimes it is just where God knows we need to be.

to the church. He said that everyone told him to slow down, but he was unwilling to do so.

A busy schedule led St. John Paul II to great suffering. Do you find yourself suffering because of a busy life? While sometimes we inflict unnecessary busyness on ourselves, sometimes a full agenda is unavoidable, inescapable. In fact, sometimes it is just where God knows we need to be. When this is the case, remember the inspiration of John Paul II, who wrote an apostolic letter on the meaning of human suffering.[21] He taught that it is worth suffering for the truth.

"Human suffering evokes compassion; it also evokes respect," he wrote. As we suffer through particularly busy passages in our lives, a mysterious undercurrent is building virtue within us. If you are experiencing the kind of busyness that is paired with suffering, remember: you are not alone. The pope wrote, suffering is "deeply rooted in humanity itself."

Suffering is "deeply rooted in humanity itself."

Miraculously, God is present with us in these moments. And may be using us to inspire someone else.

Who knows why we suffer from busyness? It could be a test, helping me become aware of stamina or virtues I didn't know I had. Or it could be an invitation to share in the experience Christ had himself on the cross. Perhaps God is allowing this suffering so we will learn how utterly dependent we are upon God for everything. Perhaps we will grow in trust in God since we cannot change the situation. It's not something we may ever understand, but remember the line from Ecclesiastes, which tells us seasons come and go, or to put it another way: "This, too, shall pass."

---

[21] Salvifici Doloris, given at Rome, at St. Peter's, on the liturgical memorial of Our Lady of Lourdes, February 11, 1984, in the sixth year of his pontificate.

St. Paul offers this in 1Cor10:13, "God is faithful and will not let you be tried beyond your strength, but with the trial God will also provide a way out, so that you may be able to bear it."

Moments of suffering are the very times to redouble your prayer efforts, even though you feel like doing the opposite.

Inspired to move?

I know a life coach whose advice for busy people is to move. Literally. Change apartments, or homes. Change cities. While this is a radical solution, this tongue-in-cheek suggestion may offer some genuine relief for busy people. You have to let go of stuff, and it frees up space in your life.

When she and her husband moved from one coast to the other, and then back again a few years later, the couple had to let go of many things or pay exorbitant moving fees. When several other moves compounded the letting go experience, this life coach realized that much of the accumulated stuff in her life was extraneous to the couple's happiness.

Our plants, pots, book and music collections, wardrobe, and other material goods may be weighing us down. As difficult as it is, letting go of accumulations frees up mental space in our lives while it clears out closets. The old saying, "you can't take it with you," is true. Some of us hang on to material objects as an attempt to feel security. As you give things away, you may find a growing sense of trust in God to provide for your needs. What you take with you into the hereafter is the relationship you have built up with God and the love you have shown to others.

> *As difficult as it is, letting go of accumulations frees up mental space in our lives while it clears out closets.*

If you have a date with yourself to do some spring-cleaning, allow yourself to give the time to God, reminding yourself that you belong to God; you are not a slave to your belongings. Talk to God while you go through your possessions, and if you can give things away, do so as St. Francis did—renounce their control over you. *Letting go is prayer.*

Inspiration can come in strange places

Yes, *things* can be very inspiring. The grandeur of mountains, a work of art, and a piece of music are all examples of inspiration for prayer. Be grateful for them. Just don't allow them to control you. Things can reveal deeper truths to us. Be open to inspiration whenever it comes.

For example, during a visit to the Boeing museum in Washington, I learned that the 787 aircraft is made primarily of composites. Do you know what makes composites strong? It's the crisscrossing of fibers. Alone, a single strand isn't very sturdy. But weave it into a matrix, suffuse it with resins, and you have a fuselage of an aircraft flying close to 300 people across a continent.

I thought about the people who crisscross my day, and how relationships strengthen us.

Another way this image inspired me was by inviting me to see the day itself as a composite material. What about you: can you create a composite using the thin strands of your day's moments and experiences? We underestimate our own strength at prayer. We also underestimate the power of prayer.

And evil wants you to expect no miracles, to think little of yourself, and underestimate the good that you accomplish. Alone, our strands of prayer may not seem like much, but link them into a daily habit, or with the intercession of a prayer partner, and watch God work.

Please never forget how valuable you are in the sight of God, who uses the weak strands of your efforts and composes something strong and lasting. Never forget you are loved.

One helpful concept for busy people is to begin noticing the little things that draw you, like water soaking into a sponge, to peace of mind. Clearly God is at work when genuine peace is present.

You, too, are inspiration

One way of taking inspiration from God is to spend some time thinking about God's qualities. What if you were to prepare a recognition dinner, a roast, for God?

Imagine what you would say in giving the toast to the Guest of Honor. Picture who else gets up to speak after you. Who is in the audience? Think about Jesus laughing at the event, listening to the generous praise of so many grateful colleagues. God loves to be thanked. Imagine someone getting up at God's recognition dinner to offer thanks.

At last the final speaker sits down, and Jesus now stands to address the assembly. What does he say? What do you hear?

Now change the honoree. What would Christ say at *your* recognition dinner?

You may not know this, but you are an inspiration to others. You say a kind word to a stranger at the store. Or during a business meeting you demonstrate honesty and integrity. You may never know who takes inspiration from you. You may never know who is listening.

> *You may never know who takes inspiration from you.*
> *You may never know who is listening.*

Who are the strangers who will cross your path today and what are their stories? You can affect their lives, and it doesn't take much—not even an audible word.

Actions are prayers.

While commuting to work by train, for example, I used to share the parts of the newspaper I didn't read with some man across the aisle. I knew nothing about him, except that I noticed one day how he snatched up each section as I tossed it onto the luggage rack between the aisles. So I just started smiling and handing them straight to him. Who was he? Who knows. But I was inspired to a loving action for that stranger on the train.

Prayer is like salt: a little can go a long way in your life and in the lives of others. Sprinkle some prayer in your life and that seasoning will permeate your whole day.

Chapter 10

Recovering from rushed moments

A busy woman writes, "I have learned that there's no use in waiting for things to slow down; it's counterproductive. Instead, I do best when I just learn how to live with the pace as it is. My frequent prayer is, 'Lord! Please help me to get done the things I need to get done, and not to worry about the rest!'"

At certain times in our lives, an overly full life just cannot be avoided. A prayer like the one above helps speed recovery from a demanding schedule that drains every ounce of energy.

Our lives and hearts are not beyond help, even if we might imagine them to be when we feel sad, doubtful, or discouraged. God has taken our hearts into the Sacred Abyss of charity and they are embers even when we do not recognize them as such. [22] Without realizing it, we may be a catalyst for starting a new fire in someone else.

Somewhere in the midst of all the rushing we do, we need to be guided by God's will for our lives and for the world. We need to have hearts desiring to do God's bidding.

---

[22] The Abyss of Charity is a name for God used by St. Catherine of Siena, the first female doctor of the church, who was born in 1347. She was the 23rd of 25 children and lived at home. How did she ever find time to pray in such a busy (or should I say full) household?

Learn to appreciate that full feeling

It is just possible that your life is not busy at all.

Actually, your life is full. That is very different. Fullness implies a cup running over with blessings. Being full is the feeling you get after a carefully prepared gourmet meal, complete with a scrumptious dessert. Full is when you are so happy you can barely stand it a second longer, and you either have to tell someone about it or cry tears of gladness.

Can we start thinking of our busy lives as full?

That three-quarters empty glass is actually a quarter full.

Why not give up responding like a bee buzzing about, busy busy busy? Why not admit our blessings, and revel in the fact that our lives are full? We have much to be grateful for in these lives full of activity. Rejoice in the fullness.

> *Can we start thinking of our busy lives as full?*

And the next time someone asks, "How are you doing?" respond with, "My life is full." And smile.

Perhaps thinking of your life as full will help clear up an unrealistic vision you may hold regarding what is *really* important. It is difficult to decipher what is most critical when rushing from one activity to the next, trying to shoehorn one more errand or task into the next minute.

"You fool! This night your life will be required of you!" warns a parable of Jesus (Luke 12:20).

We have no guarantees that tomorrow will be ours to spend. So today take a moment to thank God, to be still, even for one moment. Think about what you would do differently today if you knew it was your last day on earth.

Maybe a whole list of things will come to your mind (call a friend, pick a flower, apologize, laugh for no reason, or savor a Bible verse, for example). Pick at least one thing from your list and DO IT. Now. And then thank God for the opportunity to have done it.

Before you reject the previous paragraph's activity as "one more thing to do" in an already busy day, dig a little deeper, and you may discover a new way to unlock the network of frustrated emotions which robs you of feeling at peace within a full life.

It is important to remember to go gently with yourself—something busy people don't always do. You can ask for help and support from others, too. Jesus did. When he performed the miracle of the multiplication of loaves and fishes, he asked the apostles to help get it organized. A worshipping community is a place to find support, courage, strength, an understanding heart, and all kinds of gifts from the Holy Spirit, shared freely with us through other people.

Pressure to do more and be more often drives a busy person to attempt the impossible, rushing from one task or activity to the next. Things "fall off the plate," get jumbled, or are sloppily done. This can lead to despair and, ultimately, destruction. It's good to remember that the human body physically suffers when it undergoes stress. We need rest. Prayer is a kind of rest. The spirit within suffers when we omit prayer and don't give ourselves moments free from activity.

How can we recover when our full lives steal all of our energy and enthusiasm?

We need to allow ourselves time off from the pressure that a full life can impose. We must never give up on prayer.

Worry: the opposite of trust

Energy evaporates when we worry. Sometimes people are busy because they believe that by doing more, they can eliminate or run from what they are worrying about. Why do I find it difficult to give worries over to God? Some days I seem able to trust God to handle things, but on other days, worries seem to be attached to a bungee cord. We think we have thrown our worries off a high bridge, but suddenly they bounce wildly back into our lives again. If we don't let go, we will be on a harrowing journey off the bridge of peace.

Ask God to sever the bungee cords that hold your concerns to you.[23] Allow the worries to fall into the abyss that is God.

How do birds soar and make something as difficult as flight look so easy? Wings spread, they drift with what appears to be no effort. They were created to do that. We were created to trust in God. Can we drift on God's breath?

Many busy people wake in the night and worry. Is there a way to soften this? Anxious thoughts seem to be waiting in the wee hours. But one busy executive has a different view. When he wakes up in the middle of the night he feels glad! "Hooray," he thinks. "I don't have to get up yet!" He pulls the covers closer and gently gives God thanks for that fact again and again. If sleep does not return, he continues to thank God for this special time of being together.

> *Be anxious for nothing."*
> *(Philippians 4:6)*

---

[23] St. Catherine of Siena in her book, "The Dialogue," uses the image of a bridge to describe Christ himself. The Father sent his son to bridge the gap between heaven and earth. Christ is the way: "Run with eager longing across the bridge of Christ crucified!" She also refers to God as the Sea of Peace, with us like fish in it.

Several Scripture passages encourage this path: "Be anxious for nothing" (Philippians 4:6) and "Don't lose heart! Persevere!" (to paraphrase Hebrews 12:1-3).

An 80-year-old disabled woman whose health problems make six straight hours of rest impossible provides an example of how to pray when tempted to worry. When she can't sleep, she starts a Hail Mary for each person on her prayer list. As a mother of eight and great-grandmother of many, her list is long. And then she begins praying for friends and those in need. Some nights she says three or four full rosaries. She is an inspiration. Her lack of sleep transforms into a blessing for those who she loves, rather than being something that feeds anxiety.

Making a list of people you wish God to protect distracts one from the illusion that human life is under human control. In the movie, *White Christmas*, Bing Crosby sang: "When I'm worried and I can't sleep, *I count my blessings instead of sheep* and I fall asleep counting my blessings."

Back up a second. Rather than waiting until 3 a.m., we can turn over our subconscious minds to Christ right as we get into bed. Rather than just giving God your worries, fears, anxieties, and problems, try giving God the whole of it: "Lord, as this day ends, I give you my entire mind, all my ideas, my thoughts, and my desires. Hold them during this night, and during my sleeping hours, let me think

> *"Into your hands I commend my spirit."*
> Luke 23:46

as you would think." Try developing a habit just before going to sleep of asking God to take charge of your memories, understanding, and will. Picture a blank movie screen and concentrate on the center of the screen as you put your head on your pillow. Or just repeat Christ's words on the cross: Into your hands I commend my spirit" (Luke 23:46).

Rest is a great prescription for recovering from lives that are too full. Make sure you get plenty of it. God designed us with a built-in need to rest. So accept the gift.

When worry begins to become a consuming force, it is time to simplify. When a busy nurse I know is eaten by worries, she simply repeats, "Jesus, I trust in you" over and over, "even if I don't feel like it," she says. She knows that prayer doesn't have to be fancy. Even mentally repeating, "Oh my God, oh my God" in an attitude of abandonment is a wonderful, effective, simple prayer for people whose lives are full. Prayer doesn't need to be complicated to be valuable.

Remind yourself to leave the worry to the atheists. Make a conscious choice to grab onto faith, even when it is more of a decision than a feeling.

Simply repeating

Were you taught in elementary school to repeat something? A saying as old as Latin reminds us that "repetition is the mother of learning." Something repeated often is easier to invite to resurface later. When you find an inspiring phrase or beautiful thought, repeat it. Again and again.

As people rush, their thoughts, too, may be rushing about, seeking a place of solace. A memorized, encouraging phrase may reappear just when you need it. So take time to repeat a loving idea or thought.

Here is an example: I was reading the first letter from St. John and the second verse grabbed me: "*SEE* what *love* the Father has bestowed on us in *letting* us be called children of God. Indeed, that is what we are." [24]

---

[24] 1John3:1.

I found myself repeating a few of the words until they became a rhyme:

See what love—what love—what love

Freely bestowed on me, on us.

See what love—what love—what love

Freely bestowed on me, on us.

See what love—what love—what love

Freely bestowed on me, on us.

Soon I could carry this thought of unconditional love into the actions of my day. I walked to its cadence. When weariness hit some hours later, these words bounced into my brain, reminding me of the grace offered to me in an unfathomable and limitless love. ("See what love—what love—what love ... Freely bestowed on me, on us.")

Where *did* that thought come from? It came from a previous, simple investment of time to repeat and to pray. I was refreshed. I received a gift to balance out my weariness.

Give yourself pause

As mentioned in chapters 8 and 9, a way to subtract from a full life is to take a few moments for imaginative prayer. If you sit at a desk for long periods of time, you can set your computer or watch or phone alarm to buzz at a specific time each day. When it sounds, close your eyes. Put your mind in a different place, even if it's just for a few seconds.

If a specific meditation was fruitful for you, go back to it again. For me, one idea I go back to again and again is God as a river, described in chapter 8 (*walking on water*).

I visualize myself walking alongside God, the river. Try it. See yourself standing on the shore, edging closer to the water. Stroll along with God, letting your toes adjust to the coolness. Venture further. Your knees and thighs begin to feel the water, which feels colder as you wade deeper. It's not so bad. You get acclimated. You pause. What do you see? Is God speaking with you or are you together in silence?

I hesitate to wade in up to my belly button. Experience tells me it will be less than pleasant when the temperature shock hits my midsection. I feel the pressure to move and the power of the water begins to overtake my control.

I ask God, "Why don't I trust you more with my tender spots? Why am I afraid of suffering and pain? Why is it easier for me to embrace the Resurrected Jesus than Crucified One?"

Pray for the grace to go deeper with God, to trust more. Pray for the willingness to inch closer to God's vision for your life. Give your rushing moments to the rushing river.

The gift of listening

As people rush, the natural tendency is to listen less. A Greek philosopher coined the saying, "We have one mouth and two ears," so we should listen more and speak less. People long to be heard.

At Christ's baptism and again at the Transfiguration, God called us to pay attention to Christ. "This is my beloved Son. *Listen to Him.*"

During prayer, do I do all the talking? Or do I listen to Jesus? And in listening, do I believe more deeply? Believing means trusting, which means I am not doing all the work. I am resting in the promise that God will take care of things.

It's not easy to trust. I need to proactively grab the corners of my mind and increase the trust I have in the God who really can keep the whole universe in motion without my assistance.

> *Take a moment to listen.*

Taking a moment to listen is one way to add an extra helping of trust in God when you need it most. And trust is what we usually need, because its opposite (fear) can feed the uncomfortable, busy feeling. When fear subsides, you may feel more capable or more at peace with all that needs to be done and all the pressures leaning upon you.

See if you can listen to the attitude of Psalm 1. It offers a position of strength anchored by deep roots: "Happy those who are like a tree planted near streams of water that yields its fruit in season; its leaves never wither." Listen for God's voice, which never leads into fear. Imagine the roots of your thoughts reaching deeply into God. Believe that those who trust in the Lord will find that "whatever they do prospers."

Busy as an excuse

Sometimes I hide behind "too busy" as an excuse to decline someone's invitation to get involved in some new project. I hate to admit that I am disinterested in their cause, and it's easier to say, "I'm too busy." Is this a little white lie to protect someone's feelings? The world is not as busy as people claim it to be. I'm less than authentic when I say, "I'm too busy" in some instances.

Perhaps we are not as busy as we are in the habit of saying we are. Yet hearing ourselves saying it, we begin to believe it all the more. It's like adding a colored filter over a camera lens; everything takes on a different hue. The more I hear myself saying, "I'm too busy," the more I envision my world as frenetically out of control.

Can I stop thinking of myself as too busy, and start thinking of myself as a person who has plenty of time?

A friend I hadn't seen in 18 years picked me up at the airport when I flew to attend a high school reunion. "What would you like to do?" she asked, "because we have plenty of time."

We did? Her comment took me by surprise. I didn't see it that way. I felt pressed for time already, wondering about getting some lunch, checking into a hotel, seeing the old campus, visiting some of our old haunts in town, connecting with my husband arriving separately, and dressing for the gala. As she drove away from the airport, my chum proceeded to list a wide range of alternative ideas for ways we could spend our time. After each suggestion, she repeated, "We have plenty of time."

Pretty soon, I began to believe it.

Maybe I should try this with other ideas, planting a thought into the soil of my mind, until it grows on me more and more, and I begin to believe even more deeply that

- *"God never stops thinking of me" and*
- *"God has a beautiful plan for my life" and*
- *"I need not rush; all will be well."*

Soon I may realize that, to accomplish what God wants of me, I have plenty of time. I find consolation in Psalm 23 again: "The Lord is my shepherd; there is nothing I lack."

I lack nothing, including enough time. I have enough time in my full life to accomplish what God hopes for me.

Chapter 11

The speeding train: Forgiving moments

Clang, clang, clang. The semaphore begins to descend and I think, "uh oh. I'm caught at the train tracks again. A split second earlier and I could've been that car ahead of me who just slipped through."

Now I am forced to pause.

To wait.

To watch my blood pressure inch upward.

Do you live like a speeding train sometimes? I'm afraid that I barrel through town on a mission of frenetic activity. "Comin' through!" my body language shouts. "Watch out! I'm busy, and what I have to do is more important than you."

When I am in this state I don't realize that I'm asking everyone else to pause while I take precedence. Sometimes the semaphore announcing my arrival is late in dropping, and someone makes the mistake of trying to cross the track.

Enter forgiveness.

Busy people must apologize for the "me first" attitude that brings us careening carelessly into another's life.

Do you suffer from this "I'm more important, or my agenda is more important than you" syndrome? I don't always see the harm I do to others. Sometimes I become aware of the damage when it is too late, and therefore it is impossible to seek forgiveness personally or to make amends in the moment.

Forgiving is not easy

How do busy people learn to slow down or to let go of selfish agendas? How do people make amends to those who are hurt by hurry? How do we become aware that our priorities or actions clearly do not include others and inadvertently hurt people?

St. Paul offers encouragement to slowing down: "Humbly regard others as more important than yourselves" (Phil 2:3). If you think about the other person as having a more important task to complete than yours, it is easier to let them go first through the door, to spare a few minutes to listen to the rambling speech, or to do someone a favor when you really don't believe that you have the time to do so.

> *"Humbly regard others as more important than yourselves." (Phil. 2:3)*

Turning to God when we have one of those, "uh oh" moments, realizing we have hurt someone, can bring forth healing. When people grant themselves that moment to check in with God, they may gently become aware of a time where they have hurt another. God usually points such things out gently to us. We may find ourselves drawn to a new resolution, such as, "Tomorrow I will perform some kind act." Busy people need to seek God frequently for help, strength, and willingness to forgive *someone else* who harms them. In a busy world, it is inevitable that you will crash into someone else's agenda.

115

How do you feel when you are the one trying to cross in front of some other person's speeding train? When you experience this, it is easier for you to learn and empathize. Every person is loved and valued by God. When we forget that, it is easier to forget to forgive.

Unforgiveness. The spell checker on your computer doesn't even recognize it as a word. "What is this?" a little red line asks in a silent form of denial.

Funny how the world can spell animosity, revenge, retribution, and payback. Unforgiveness? That is not even a word that is recognizable to the modern computer. How ironic when the world understands and nurtures hurt and punishment.

Unforgiveness contributes to back pain, sore muscles, and other physical symptoms. When you feel sore, ask yourself, "Is my body inviting me to examine my recent history for failures to forgive someone—or myself?" God can use your body as a prayer. I mean, God can do anything.

Invite God to call attention to the "misspellings" of love in life. "Jesus, be my spell checker, and call my attention to those things where I have made a mistake by not loving."

Then take the line from the Our Father and turn it from a conditional statement into a bold declaration of intention (take out the word "as"): "**We forgive** those who trespass against us."

Can broken relationships be repaired?

Jesus is part of a family and knows the dynamics of complicated relationships. God as Trinity is a family. As children in God's family who keep messing up, we need a Brother to go to our Dad and fix things up for us. Sometimes it feels easier to go to the Mother of God first, asking her to take our prayer to her Son.

God never stops seeking us out to save us, and we are constantly in need of being saved. Especially when we think in our busy lives that we control it all.

Who are we that the God of the bluest sky and the most beautiful sites of nature never stops wanting us back? Thank God we have a Brother to look up to, who can show us the way home, through forgiveness. When forgiveness seems humanly impossible, God works a miracle and brings healing to damaged relationships.

Sometimes, it feels more natural to run to Mom because she is really good at speaking to Dad on my behalf. And Dad loves Mom so much; how can God resist when the Mother of God adds the strength of her request to our own? "Yes, dear, your beloved's request is worth hearing."

A common strategy for running from forgiving someone is to stay so busy that we don't have to think about the brokenness and pain. Just slowing down can be a prayer.

And it is not only other people we don't want to forgive. We need to forgive ourselves, to acknowledge our shortcomings, to own our failures and to admit weaknesses. That is not easy. And it can be painful.

It is not uncommon to be holding a grudge against God, who allowed to happen the circumstances that stand as roadblocks to our wishes. People may not word it this way, but we may feel that God really does not have a clue about what we are going through, nor does God care. Perhaps we just think that God doesn't bother with small, day-to-day concerns. Looking around at what is wrong with the world makes it easier to refuse to forgive God for things gone awry. We shake our heads and stop expecting God to do anything about it.

When people are busy staying angry with God, it's more difficult to create space to be with God. What might I hear?

I may be afraid of the answer. Yet to talk to God about it may be just what I need for healing. Express irritation—or any genuine feeling— in prayer.

Honestly, do you really think you could say anything to God that God doesn't already see inside your heart? So you might as well talk to God about your aggravation. Be nice about it, as you would in a polite conversation with a respected colleague. But freely express your issues. When you express your attitudes in prayer, surprising pathways to new vistas can open up.

> *Do you really think you could say anything to God that God doesn't already see inside your heart?*
>
> *So you might as well talk to God about your aggravation.*

Another factor in being busy could be that a great deal of energy is going into holding on to past hurts and legitimate reasons for refusing to forgive. After all, the world is full of injustice.

God didn't invite us to forgive only when people deserve it. God asks us to be magnanimous about forgiveness. We need to let go *especially* when the offending party doesn't deserve it.

Who do you most need to forgive in your life?

Perhaps you feel afraid to ask yourself this question because you really don't want to let go. Perhaps it is more comfortable just to stay busy and avoid thinking about it.

Have I been here before?

Sometimes being busy feels like running in a hamster wheel. No progress is made as the same ground is traversed yet again. God allows us to choose freely, and sometimes we are choosing to rehash, relive, and avoid taking a step toward forgiveness. I haven't learned my lesson.

If I can stop running, perhaps a new insight will occur. It takes a lot of energy to keep running, especially if I am avoiding forgiveness. It takes more energy to hold on to a grudge than to let it go and put it behind me.

In granting creation free choice, God permits us to both withhold and grant forgiveness. One way off the hamster wheel, a way out of the cage, is to embrace forgiveness both for ourselves and others.

Ruminate. That's the word for what cows do—chewing food, cud, over and over again. We do this too, regurgitating partially digested actions/thoughts and chewing on them or reliving them again and again. Forgiving is more of a forgetfulness of the hurtful actions, the carelessly spoken words and the painful memories. Let us "swallow our pride."

What if one of the ways in which we are an image of God is forgetfulness? After all, God promises not to remember our sins. Psalm 103:11-12 says, "... so great is God's mercy toward those who fear God; as far as the east is from the west, so far has God removed our transgressions from us." What a relief. And Micah 7:19 refers to God's sea of forgetfulness: "God will again have compassion on us, and will subdue our iniquities. God will cast all our sins into the depths of the sea." And then God posts a sign for us that says, "NO FISHING."

> *What if one of the ways in which we are an image of God is forgetfulness?*

Starting fresh is made possible when we forgive. We must forgive ourselves the action-packed schedules that prevent love from being the overarching motivator.

Forgiveness leads to healing and opening new opportunities. Perhaps it points to a new road, to discovering that to which the busy person is really called.

These are tough topics

Will I *ever* be able to forgive? A school teacher told me that the *Wizard of Oz* gives a good insight into what to do when temped to despair for whatever reason—perhaps because there's too much to do or because of unresolved hurt. Discouragement disguises itself as a good thing, just as lying down to sleep among the flowers was an attractive but potentially lethal option for Dorothy on her road to the Emerald City. This teacher advises: "If you find yourself getting weary in a field of poppies, get up and run! Don't wallow in the poppies."

In other words, do not be tricked, sidetracked, or distracted by a false light—the beam at the end of the tunnel that is really an oncoming train. This teacher is talking about Christ's invitation to walk in the true light, which *never* discourages us.[25]

Avoid misinterpreting the shadows as interesting, attractive paths to investigate and dwell in. Do not be deceived by the dark. Your home is not there. Happiness isn't there. Don't dawdle with discouragement. It is one of the detractors on the road to joy. Take some action opposite the desire to despair. When evil whispers to give up, that is especially when you want to run to prayer, whether that means making an act of your will to forgive or unloading your discouragement on God in honest, heartfelt prayer.

Another danger exists: to mistake that field of poppies as the end goal instead of the Emerald City. The opiate of a

---

[25] 1 John 1:7 "... if we walk in the Light as he himself is in the Light, we have fellowship with one another, and the blood of Jesus His Son cleanses us from all sin."

distracting path or activity can overcome you, just as it did Dorothy and her friends just outside of Oz. Expect to be sidetracked through no fault of your own, but admit your need for God's saving power.

The pilgrims to Oz got out of the poppy fields because the good fairy intervened. Similarly, we need to depend upon the super-strength of God to save us. We can ask for help as well as recognize that God does intervene in human history. And ask others to pray for and encourage you.

It's not so easy, is it? Self- condemnation and self-doubt can keep us from moving out of a tough spot. Sometimes I wallow in my sins instead of accepting God's grace to start fresh and give myself a break. After all, we were made to know, love, praise, and serve God, who loves us, flaws and all. Thank God that God is not interested in punishment. Discipline, yes, and fortitude, yes. God wants us to ask for what we need.

We need to forgive ourselves when we don't measure up to our own standards. And we need to forgive others, too.

There is a story about St. Ignatius slacking the reins of his mount in a moment of indecision, vacillating between taking a path of revenge to chase after someone, or choosing to take the other fork. He thought he would let the horse decide, and the horse ambled away from the path of revenge.

Perhaps we need to ask the Lord to help us to slack the reins on our lives. Let God lead to a path of forgiveness.

Dark moments

People who pray inevitably come upon moments of dryness. Dark times are a normal part of a prayer life. Saints like John of the Cross describe times when it feels as if God is absent. St. Teresa of Calcutta experienced this, too. If God feels far away,

> **At times like these, do the opposite.**

what have you got to hang on to but faith? In moments where you can't feel God's presence, the temptation is to give up praying, or abandon habits developed during inspired moments. At times like these, *do the opposite*: spend a few *more* moments in prayer. The loneliness may be unrelenting. You may feel as if no one can understand your private pain. Don't give up.

Thankfully, Jesus is perfectly capable of taking on the pain and suffering in our lives. Christ is present when we hang on the cross of the day that isn't so joyful. Christ thirsts with us and hurts with us. Jesus takes on our pain. It may feel as if these dark days will last forever. In faith, claim the truth that they will not.

God may be asking you to continue walking on a path that is overwhelming. God invites you to take the Almighty's hand. Divine help is always there, even when we don't see or feel it.

Fear nothing

Don't be afraid to pray that God would show you the day according to the way God sees it. Yes, we may discover personal shortcomings or see the consequences of our sins. We may encounter a lack of humility or self-deception. But God shows us these things with a gentle, loving hand, just as a parent gently wipes the grimy hands of a child who decided to play in the mud. If we are trying to live good lives,

> **God doesn't lead us into discouragement or despair...**

God doesn't lead us into discouragement or despair over our failings. God stands ready to forgive as soon as we ask. God may ask us to help clean up the messes we've made, and that may take some time. The Almighty can overcome any obstacle easily, if God chooses to.

Don't be afraid to ask for help. Try this:

Oh, Jesus! What could I do without you!

Where would I be?

I fall upon your infinite Mercy and compassion.

Oh, Divine Assistance! Come to my aid.

While certain tasks that keep us busy may pull us from the very things that bring us fulfillment or healing—from our true path—we must not give up. When the long list is only half done at the end of the day, and what you hoped to accomplish is a drip next to the torrent of to-do's, don't give in to the temptation to stop trying. Turn it over to God once again.

It's such a little thing...

God doesn't expect us to call for help only in big things. God takes care of the bacteria, too. No concern of ours is too small for God, who is Lord of all, and worthy to receive our every circumstance.

Little wounds can become infected and make us really sick. If an unforgiven wound saps your energy, take it to God in a simple conversation. Remember that Christ was unjustly treated and can pray with you, "Father forgive them." Tell God how you really feel. God can take it. Christ suffered all kinds of things and forgave in love. Christ can teach us to love and forgive, too.

It takes divine grace to love as God loves. It may mean being ridiculed, humbled, and disparaged. It may be an invitation to stand bravely at the foot of Christ's cross.

All of us are failures in some ways, and God loves us anyway. That love is more powerful than my anger, self-recrimination, and false evaluation from others. It is a love inviting us to be compassionate and kind first of all with ourselves. Let us ask for the grace to listen only to God's evaluations of us.

Tempted to give up

Remember that Jesus was tempted. When you feel you are just too busy to pray, ask yourself if it is a temptation to leave a fruitful habit. You may be tempted to give up. Don't give in!

Jesus' mission was not an easy one. He struggled with the same things we do: what truly matters in human life. His mission was urgent, and therefore he understands when we are busy with our own urgent concerns.

To be human is to be tempted to digress from centering our lives on God. "I know best," is my unspoken attitude, sometimes unconsciously.

And I think I have to do it all on my own power. I forget miracles. The exact time I need to toss up a simple prayer is when I have too much to do. It's enough of a prayer just to remember that God is in control; not a time to set God aside.

What should we do when tempted? Pray. Especially when you have no time. Pray when you are too busy. Pray when you feel like skipping it. Pray for strength. Ask God to meet you. Run to the One who was tempted, just like you are, and pray.

> *Pray for strength. Ask God to meet you.*

I am frequently in awe of the ways that God comes to my assistance when I acknowledge my powerlessness over the temptation that is hounding me. Sometimes all I can pray is, "Jesus. Jesus! Jesus." And do you know what? It's a great and effective prayer. It's enough.

The guest is waiting

When you hear the doorbell or someone knocking on your door, do you ignore it? What if you are expecting company? Do you make them wait? Of course not.

So why would you ask Christ to keep waiting outside your heart? He already knocked. He is already at your door. You are being invited to forgive and let go.

Rush to the barriers to God's grace and fling them aside to make room for the Prince of Peace. Invite Jesus in. And if he calls you to go out to meet him, do not hesitate. Go! Don't let past mistakes hold you back. There is <u>nothing</u> we've done that God can't forgive.

My refusal to forgive and my fears of inadequacies are roadblocks to trust. But I don't need to keep Christ waiting. God forgives my shortcomings and helps me to forgive those who have disappointed me.

> *There's <u>nothing</u> we've done that God can't forgive. you.*

Rush into Christ's waiting arms. You have no reason to fear. Here is one circumstance when you should rush!

God always keeps our best interests in mind. God plans wonderful things for us, and persistently knocks. God is always there, waiting patiently.

In conclusion: Where did the time go?

What? You made it all the way here? (or are you so busy that you *started* here? I often jump to conclusions myself.)

By now you know that I believe all of life can be a prayer. Love is a verb, and love is prayer. The secret of prayer for busy people lies in remembering that prayer is God's project, and we are willing participants. We grow in enjoying the fleeting prayer moments and inspirations of our lives by becoming more aware, living intentionally, being gentle (not judgmental) with ourselves and others, and forming new habits.

Do you really think that the God of all time couldn't stretch today for you if God wanted to? Look at how the sun danced at Fatima, Portugal, on October 13, 1917. Thousands and thousands of people witnessed it. So invest a few moments in time dedicated to God because God can change the upcoming circumstances of your day, especially the ones that give you heart palpitations at the thought of them.

Remember that Christ walked on water (John 6:19), a seemingly impossible feat for a human. Christ can do impossible things for us, too. Miracles don't occur only in history. They happen every day.

> *Christ can do impossible things for us, too.*

Recall that faith can move mountains (Matthew 17:20). Sometimes the mountain we need to move requires some impossible stretching of time. Or an extra set of helping hands. Perhaps someone shows up when we least expect it and helps lift some part of our load. God is known for using this method of intervention to assist us to "stretch time."

God can do the opposite too. Especially during meditation, a half hour can slip past. So relax and expect a miracle. You never know what God has in mind.

> *Relax. You never know what God has in mind.*

Prayer doesn't occur only in silent times, in churches, or when we feel holy. Prayer doesn't have to be difficult, boring, restrictive or restrained. Experiment with your own creative ways to pray.

There are as many ways to pray as there are people.

Prayer is relationship building. It's how God and I get to know one another. It's how God helps me discover my true self. There is a natural longing to be together.

And prayer is an *adventure*. We set out, not really knowing how things will end. It's a step forward into something mysterious. Find your own style. You CAN find God in all things. Your personal experience can provide you with genuine encounters with God.

Some say life is a journey. I say life is prayer. All of life can be prayer. Jesus said, "I am The Way." We are people of The Way, and the way is adventurous. Something wonderful is just around God's corner. It may feel risky, or new, and possibly exciting. It includes accepting who we are, flaws and all. God knows we are this way.

As Pope Benedict XVI said on All Saints Day, 2011, to become saints means to fulfill completely what we already are. And what we are is children of God. As children, we are beloved, whether we are busy or not.

Appendix

Sample prayers for busy people

In this section are some sample prayers and prayer starters designed to provide inspiration or a starting point for your own thriving relationship with God. Remember that you are not in charge. God is. Give yourself time to see what God has in mind.

God, all I have is a couple of loaves and two fish.
But it is enough!
I trust in you, God, that it will multiply.
And I am not responsible for—or in charge of—the miracle,
or if no miracle appears.
Let me be at peace with whatever happens.
Thank you.

"You are lovable."
Today is our gift:
Your gift to me, God.
My gift to you.
You.

Lord, as I begin a new day, bracing for the crosses and hoping for joys ahead, let me remember to be thankful. I begin by giving you thanks for all good things: for the weather, a good night's rest, a car that works, an inspiring word from another, for music. So many reasons to praise your Holy Name! And grant me the grace to be thankful for the difficult things, too, for they will inevitably come to challenge me.

Lord, I dedicate myself to you today—without reserve.
I promise to trust in you, and to love.
Help me remember to listen for your voice in every situation.
I choose you today,
with all my heart,
and I will serve you,
even if it seems that all the results of my labor are ash.
I will pray every moment
by dedicating NOW all I think, say, and do to you.
And when I notice, through your grace,
that I have strayed from mindfulness of you,
I will run back to the desert of prayer and seek you,
or rather, wait to rediscover myself in you,
where I belong, where I have always been.

I'm going to sit here, God, where you can see me.

Jesus,

Some days are harder than others.

My to-do list seems interrupted a thousand times, and what I wanted to accomplish falls by the wayside. Help me to learn that your to-do list is the most important one.

I know your priorities for me are:

1. Love God.

2. Love myself.

3. Love others.

4. Love when it is easy.

5. Love when it is difficult.

6. Love at all times.

Help me remember that this to-do list is enough.

Breathe in me, breath of God.
Fill me with life anew.
That I might want the things you want,
and do what you would do.

Amen. Alleluia.

To be repeated until the words flow, one into another:

I am

The Way

Yahweh

Jesus says I am the Way

Yahweh

You are

The Way.

Light my torch and keep it burning.

Satisfy my constant yearning

for your love and all it's earning.

Nothing is as marvelous as being a vessel for you,
Oh Mighty God.

To be filled with your Holy Presence, to be a delicate instrument in your hand, is the most delightful experience. I melt into a new form of being so that you can permeate me, and move in me, and move me. I lose myself in you, just as a thin glass cylinder, open at both ends, disappears under water.

You flow through, and still I retain my independence.

Yet I am lost in you, unseen but present. I am contained,
immersed, and cleansed.
I am a conduit for your infinite, flowing love.

Oh, to be lost in you, Love!

Oh that others may see only you
and not be distracted by the glass cylinder.

Help me, Lord.

I feel like I am running so hard,
and shouting over my shoulder to you,

and still I run

away,

as if I could find the answers myself.

Help me, Lord. What am I running TO?
What am I running FROM?

Oh, God, why does it feel like you leave us alone down here?

Thank you, God, for my mother, for your mother. for music. for cute babies. for laughter. for presents. for coffee. for toilet paper. for plants. for warmth. for silence. for alarm clocks. for clean towels. for showers. for birds singing. for a good night's rest. for mail. for books. for magazines. for computers. for fingernails. for photography. for rain. for friends. for what I should have listed first: thank you for Jesus Christ!

Companion Holy Spirit.
You are leading me every step of the way.

And you know the next step.

Creative God who made the universe,
please make something good and creative out of today.

Brother Jesus,
whisper into the busy life I lead,
that I may be aware of your directing guidance and example.

Jesus, I feel like I skipped a day.
Life is screaming past—in a rush—like flood waters.
More rain expected today.

If I am going to avoid being washed away,
I must sink my roots deeply in you, Jesus.

I've only got a minute, God.
What are you thinking right now?
"I wish she would slow down?"
Be my inspiration!

God speaks: Watch Me.

See My sunrise.

See all my brave people entering another day—
some at difficult jobs—one foot, then another.

I am a humble God.

I respond: Lord, you are a marvel to me,

For I am NOT humble.

You are willing to create a sunrise just for your delight in it.
It is okay with you if no one notices.
And I? How I long to be noticed!

I want to be recognized, encouraged, lauded, thanked,
and repaid for my accomplishments.

The sunrise is silent, but its colors beautifully shout,
"see what God made!"

Lord, help me to watch for you today.

And help me not fear being overlooked.
Help me to be open to humility.

I will not remain in the briar of revenge.

    I will move into the desert of prayer.

I will not choose the quagmire of despair.

I will move into the desert of prayer.

I will not stagnate in the pool of self pity.

I will move into the desert of prayer.

I will not cultivate the thorn bushes of gossip, slander, name-calling, sullen silence, or outrage.

I will move into the desert of prayer.

Repeat, under your breath and in tune with your breath:

Abba. Yeshwah. Ruah.

Abba is the Aramaic word for Father. Yeshwah is a phonetic spelling for the way Jesus' name may have been pronounced. Ruah is the Hebrew word for breath or spirit, and the Holy Spirit.

I find these three words for the Holy Trinity blend well into a prayer that quiets my busy mind and helps me to slow down. I start with whispering Abba as I inhale. I exhale Yeshwah. I inhale Ruah. I then slow down a bit more. I take both a breath in and a breath out to whisper Abba. I do the same for each name. I try to disengage my mind from all thoughts and distractions. See if you can take two full breaths in and out to say each name.

Slow down.

Thank God you were busy, too, Jesus.

Can you help me walk on water today, too?

You invite me to expect miracles when I reflect on your life.

We've got a lot to do today, you and I.

Or is it that I *think* you want me to do these things,
when really you have a less action-packed agenda
in mind for me than I do?

Help me make the necessary course corrections today
that I might stay on track with your plan for me. Amen!

It is time for me to fall asleep, Lord.

I pray for the gift of being able to see the day just past
as you saw it.

Where did you walk with me today?

Where did I see Jesus, your son?

Thank you, God, for all the blessings which come to my memory.

Show me your action in this day, especially where
I may have overlooked it.

I ask forgiveness
for the ways I fell short of what you hoped for me.

Thank you for gently showing these things to me.

Before I know it, God, it will be tomorrow.
And it, too, if it comes for me, will be a gift.

I know you will be there, ready to give me strength and courage.

Tomorrow is a new day. I gently let go of today.

I place all of me in your tender care.

Amen.

Catherine of Siena, a Doctor of the Church, dictated a book titled, The Dialogue, *available online. She speaks of the special relationship God enjoys with us through the Eucharist. She relates an image of God speaking to the soul:*

> "By receiving this Sacrament she dwells in Me and I in her, as the fish in the sea, and the sea in the fish—thus do I dwell in the soul, and the soul in Me—the Sea of Peace."

How does this image lead you into prayer? What other images make it easier for you to think about the ineffable One?

(Use this space to sketch out your own heartfelt prayers. Dare to share it with a friend or relative.)

(Cover Photo: Mendocino Cliffs, by Stephen Pehanich ©)

ABOUT THE AUTHOR

Loretta Pehanich is a Catholic writer with more than 20 years' experience in ministry, including retreat teams in the Bay Area and Southern California, and 15 years in small group and Bible study leadership roles.

Loretta offers workshops on prayer for busy people, relating from her personal experience as a working woman, wife, mother, grandmother and church and community volunteer.

With a journalism degree from USC's Annenberg School of Communication, Loretta worked for a diocesan newspaper and was magazine editor at a Jesuit institution. She is also a freelance writer and blogger.

Loretta is a gifted storyteller who practiced on her four children and on her siblings before that. She continues to create stories to entertain her nine grandchildren.

A lifelong Catholic, Loretta is a spiritual director, a lector, a choir member, a former RCIA team member and volunteer with the St. Vincent de Paul Society, and an active participant in several committees and professional organizations.
But she is never too busy to pray.
She and her husband Steve reside in Sacramento, California.

Email her at LorettaKP@gmail.com.

Made in the USA
San Bernardino, CA
22 May 2018